#startupeverywhere

Startup Guide Tel Aviv

Editor: **Zoe Cooper**
Copyeditor: **Marissa van Uden**
Proofreader: **Ted Hermann**
Writers: **Josh Raisher, Mark Fletcher** and **Lisa Mallner**
Assistant: **Jenna van Uden**
Local Content Production: **Erez Gavish, Natan Leibzon, Anat Greemland, Keren Brown, Nadler Elishar & Co** and **Noya Einhorn**
Photographer: **Omer Hacohen**
Researchers: **Erez Gavish** and **Natan Leibzon**
Production Manager: **Tim Rhodes**
Design: **Ines Pedro**

Illustrations by **Joana Carvalho**

Additional photography by
Daniela Carducci and **Unsplash.com**

Printed in Tel-Aviv, Israel by
Erez Lavy Comprehensive Print Solutions
erez.lavy.productions@gmail.com

Published by **Startup Guide World IVS**
Kanonbådsvej 2, 1437 Copenhagen K
info@startupguide.world

Visit: startupguide.world

ISBN 978-3-947624-03-4

Copyright © 2017 Startup Guide World IVS All rights reserved.

Although the authors and publisher have made every effort to ensure that the information in this book was correct, they do not assume and hereby disclaim any liability to any party for any loss, damage, or disruption caused by errors or omissions, whether such errors or omissions result from negligence, accident, or any other cause. No part of this publication may be reproduced, distributed, or transmitted in any form or by any means, including photocopying, recording, or other electronic or mechanical methods, without the prior written permission of the publisher, except in the case of brief quotations embodied in critical reviews and certain other non-commercial uses permitted by copyright law.

STARTUP GUIDE TEL AVIV

STARTUP GUIDE TEL AVIV

In partnership with **TLV Starters**

Proudly Supported by

introduction

Sissel Hansen
/ Startup Guide

Since our very first Startup Guide issue back in 2014, I've been wondering if we'll one day see a Startup Guide book published outside of Europe. Back then, I was certainly attracted by the thought, but I didn't know when (or if) it would become a reality. Although it took a little longer than three years, the Startup Guide series has finally stepped into a new region – and the first stop is the Middle East.

From the very beginning, the team and I could see that the Tel Aviv guide would be a special edition; the "startup nation" has proven to be as incredible as Dan Senor and Saul Singer claimed in their infamous bestseller. The determination, hospitality and confidence of the people from Tel Aviv have been outstanding – and certainly beyond what we've often found here in Europe.

Israel's admirable commitment to innovation, combined with the quick minds, logic and lack of hierarchy in Israeli culture, have all led to Tel Aviv's thriving startup community. Hard work pays off, and Tel Avivians know it well. It might take a little longer for Tel Aviv to reach the highs of Silicon Valley or New York, but with such dedication, an extremely diverse society, and the aim to expand internationally, it is on the verge of becoming a pivotal point of entrepreneurship in tech, design, art, food, medicine and other industries within the Middle East and beyond.

The Startup Guide Tel Aviv has a strong spirit – just like the history, people and culture of Tel Aviv itself. You'll find some incredibly valuable advice in this book, coming from some fascinating and experienced founders, experts and, of course, startups. Iris Shoor, a contributor to this edition, aptly said that entrepreneurship is a challenge of "not being able to tell if I'm crazy or I'm doing something right." I hope that the guide will inspire you to feel Tel Aviv's energy too.

Sissel
CEO and Founder

foreword

Ron Huldai
/ Mayor of Tel Aviv-Yafo

Shalom,

I like to call Tel Aviv the Startup City of the Startup Nation. Over the past decade, our startup community has gained global recognition, and thanks to its hard work, Tel Aviv-Yafo is recognized as one of the most attractive cities for technological development. I believe that entrepreneurial spirit is part of our DNA.
When Tel Aviv was founded on empty sand dunes in 1909, its founders intended for it to one day be a major metropolis – "the New York of the Land of Israel," as they called it. In essence, these founders were the city's first startup entrepreneurs: They were dreamers who had a vision that nobody around them believed in. But they did not give in to skepticism, and by sticking to their dream they managed to fulfill it.

Today, a century later, the municipality invests a great deal in promoting our creative ecosystem. We do this first and foremost by investing in the city itself. I believe that creative people want to live in attractive cities. We allocate major funds to culture and art, we work tirelessly on creating fun and safe public spaces, we create policies to encourage nightlife, and we set up innovative and excellent educational and communal programs, all so that our young people stay in Tel Aviv-Yafo even after they become parents. Thanks to these efforts, the number of young people in the city has doubled in the past fifteen years, and today more than half of our population is under the age of thirty-five.

Second, we invest in promoting our entrepreneurs. In the past few years, we've set up numerous public coworking spaces, reduced taxes for early-stage startups, spread free wifi in our main public spaces, opened municipal data and have implemented many more measures to encourage and enable our startup community. We want to signal how important the creative tech community is to Tel Aviv's economy, to the city's global positioning and, most importantly, to the energetic spirit of its people.

Yours,
Ron Huldai
Mayor of Tel Aviv-Yafo

overview

Local Ecosystem

[Facts & Figures]
- Israel's economic center.
- One third of the city's residents are between the ages of eighteen and thirty-five.
- The city is small and flat, great for walking and cycling, and has over 120 km of bike trails, 14 km of beaches and averages 318 sunshine days per year.
- The airport is only fifteen minutes by train or thirty minutes by car from the city center.
- Most of the communication in startup and high-tech companies in Israel is in English, and most of the residents of the city are fluent in English.
- Top verticals: big data and cloud, fintech, cyber, IOT and adtech.
- One of the highest startup-per-capita densities in the world, with one startup for every 290 residents.
- There are nineteen startups per square kilometer.
- One in ten employees in the city are in the high-tech sector.
- Seventy-three multinational companies are located in or near the city, including Amazon, eBay, Alibaba, Google, Facebook, Samsung, Coca Cola, Yahoo!, LG, Microsoft, 3M and Deutsche Telekom.

[Notable Scaleups:]
- Gett raised **$640 million**
- Payoneer raised **$270 million**
- Outbrain raised **$194 million**
- WalkMe raised **$167 million**
- Taboola raised **$160 million**
- StoreDot raised **$126 million**
- SimiarWeb raised **$112 million**
- IronSource raised **$105 million**
- Kenshoo raised **$49 million**
- My Heritage raised **$49 million**

Funding per year

- 700 companies raised a total of **$4.4 billion** in 2015
- 659 deals worth a total of **$4.8 billion** in 2016

Sources: startupnationcentral.org, innovationisrael.mag.calltext.co.il, haaretz.com, timesofisrael.com, themarker.com, geektime.com, globes.co.il, jpost.com and Center for Economic and Social Research of Tel-Aviv Yafo Municipality

[City:] # Tel Aviv, Israel

[Statistics:] Urban Tel Aviv population: **438,818**
Surface area: **52 km²**
Percentage of residents with a post-secondary education: **57.2 percent**

Tel Aviv

Local Community Partner / TLV Starters

Often called the "City That Never Sleeps," Tel Aviv is the place for innovators and those who challenge the status quo. The local ecosystem – a dense matrix of entrepreneurs, VCs, multinational companies, programs, spaces and more – is not only fascinating but thriving. It has formed a community that has been ranked as one of the top places to grow a startup outside the US for many years now. The pace of life here is fast, people are opinionated and straightforward, business circles are quick, and the overall culture seems like it was intentionally built to grow startups.

As entrepreneurs who believe in getting things done, TLV Starters shares a passion for innovation-related projects. We're experienced with building startups and communities, crafting new products and cooperating with other players in the local and global ecosystems. Thanks to our constant curiosity and strong focus on bringing ideas to reality, showcasing the best of Tel Aviv's startup scene is a perfect fit with our agenda. Therefore, our collaboration with Startup Guide was a no-brainer and a great privilege. After all, in the age of constant digital connection, where online content can feel overwhelming (or even confusing), it's important to stop for a minute and take the time to organize our thoughts on our flourishing tech scene. And so, we wanted to create a valuable and relevant book to add to the fast-growing Startup Guide book series.

A great city deserves a great book, and in order to make one we needed to find a way to curate the best of Tel Aviv's metropolis and illustrate its diversity. It is not an easy task, as the industry is made up of thousands of startups and hundreds of talented professionals, spaces and programs. That is why we carefully chose the book's Advisory Board – all are top industry leaders of different verticals and point of views, and all put a great deal of thought and effort into selecting those featured in this book.

You now hold the result in your hands. We hope you enjoy its content, and get a chance to know and connect with the people who are devoting their lives to creating a global impact.

Erez Gavish and Natan Leibzon
Cofounders

contents

startups

Airobotics **32**

Argus Cyber Security **34**

Biocatch **36**

drupe **38**

Engie **40**

Feelter **42**

Hargol FoodTech **44**

HT BioImaging **46**

Lemonade **48**

Nexar **50**

prooV **52**

Ripples **54**

Zest **56**

programs

8200 EISP **60**

The Junction **62**

KamaTech **64**

MAOF Hybrid **66**

Microsoft Accelerator Tel Aviv **68**

SigmaLabs **70**

TechForGood **72**

Unistream **74**

contents

overview 12 essentials 18 directory 198 glossary 202 about the guide 204

spaces

AYEKA **78**
Google Campus Tel Aviv **82**
Merkspace **86**
Mindspace **90**
SOSA **94**
Spaces Oxygen **98**
WeWork **102**
WMN **106**

experts

Microsoft Israel **112**
Gett **118**
Bank Leumi **124**
IATI **130**
Reinhold Cohn Group **136**
SZ Shvarts Zedkia **142**

founders

Fiverr
/ Micha Kaufman **150**

Mellanox Technologies
/ Eyal Waldman **158**

NFX Guild
/ Gigi Levy-Weiss **166**

Oribi
/ Iris Shoor **174**

StarTAU | TAU Ventures
/ Oren Simanian **182**

TLV Partners
/ Rona Segev **190**

essentials

essentials

Tel Aviv Essentials

With sunny weather and a perfect location on the Mediterranean coastline, Israel's business capital, Tel Aviv-Yafo, is considered one of the best startup ecosystems outside the US.

Founded a little more than one hundred years ago by Jews on the outskirts of the ancient port city of Jaffa (Yafo), Tel Aviv earned its title as "the Nonstop City," "the White City," and "the Mediterranean Capital of Cool" (by the *New York Times*). In its short lifetime, Tel Aviv has developed into an international business hub and vibrant city with a population of over four hundred thousand. It forms the heart of a 3.5-million-people metropolitan area called Gush Dan.

With pluralism, tolerance and democracy as its values, people from all corners of the world can be found having a beer in the open-all-night cafes and bars, looking for bargains in Levinsky or at the Carmel markets, taking a run in Yarkon park, getting some fresh air at the old port, or simply laying their heads on the sand at one of its famous beaches. From the highrise towers of Rothschild Boulevard – a base for dozens of multinational companies and fresh startups – to quarters like the historic Neve Tzedek and trendy Florentin, the city is booming and blooming.

Before You Come 20

Cost of Living 20

Cultural Differences 20

Renting an Apartment 23

Finding a Coworking Space 23

Insurance 25

Visas and Work Permits 25

Taxes 25

Starting a Company 27

Opening a Bank Account 27

Getting Around 27

Telephone Contracts 29

Learning the Language 29

Meeting People 29

Before You Come

Moving to Tel Aviv begins with rewiring your brain to 'Israel mode,' as the way things are done there can be quite different from many other countries. The local coin is the shekel (₪), and credit cards can be used almost everywhere. The city is quite small (52 km^2), and most of the people and places are in close proximity. This makes it easy to get everywhere and meet many people in a short time. Do your research before you come with things you wish to do and see, as there is so much to experience. If you're visiting on a business trip, it is recommended to schedule meetings in advance. A "change of plans" can take place on short notice – it's common for meetings to be scheduled two hours in advance or to be postponed just two hours before taking place.

Cost of Living

Your primary expenses in Tel Aviv will be housing, food and entertainment. Monthly rent for partially furnished accommodations will range from 4,000₪ ($1,100) for a 50 m^2 flat up to 8,200₪ ($2,300) or more for a 80 m^2 flat, depending on the location and condition, etc. Utilities such as electricity, gas and water will cost about 650₪ ($190) a month. Expect internet services to cost around $25 and a cell phone package around $15 a month. It is recommend to buy groceries at local markets like the Carmel or Levinsky, where prices are relatively low and the quality is high. A basic lunchtime menu in a cafe will cost around 55₪ ($15), and a cappuccino around 13₪ ($4). Beer is quite expensive in Tel Aviv, costing around 30₪ ($8) for 500 mL. A monthly membership to a gym would cost around 275₪ ($80). Check out numbeo.com for more cost of living information.

Cultural Differences

Tel Aviv is a cosmopolitan city and home to many foreigners who move there to do business and enjoy the Mediterranean beaches. Be prepared to meet people of all religions and origins, enjoy the delicious multinational cuisine, and experience a unique mix of Western and Middle Eastern cultures. Israelis are known for being straightforward and love to share their opinions, even when not asked for it. This is a part of the informal, warm and non-hierarchical Israeli culture. The dress code is similarly informal. Ties are seldom worn (even at official meetings), and a nice pair of jeans is usually just fine. Note that most businesses are closed on *Shabbat*, which is the time period between Friday afternoon and Saturday evening. Though most cafes, restaurants and cinemas are open, be sure to check in advance whether the venue you plan to visit is open.

essentials

essentials

essentials

Renting an Apartment

As with many major cities, it's not an easy task to find a great apartment with a reasonable price tag in Tel Aviv. Begin by choosing which neighborhood you wish to live in, as there are large differences in prices, the local vibe and facilities. Be sure to check out SecretTelAviv, a portal for English speakers that posts listings for apartments, or check out other listing websites like yad2.co.il, winwin.co.il, komo.co.il or madlan.co.il. Usually, the landlord will announce an 'open house' event for people who wish to check out the place. Make sure you show up ahead of time, as good deals will be taken quickly. Most landlords will ask for checks for the whole lease contract in advance, plus a deposit check and one or two guarantors to cover any accidental damage to the apartment.

See **Flats and Rentals** page **200**

Finding a Coworking Space

Tel Aviv has hundreds of coffee shops that also serve as temporary offices for thousands of entrepreneurs, freelancers, writers and dreamers. But over the past few years, the coworking scene has exploded with new, cool spaces. Most office spaces can be found on websites like spacing.com or pickspace.net. They usually offer printing services, coffee, snacks, a mailing address and sometimes even a swimming pool and gym. Some spaces attract specific types of members to create a unique mix of renters, in accordance with the place's vision. It's also recommended to schedule a tour to get the look and feel of the place. All coworking spaces offer monthly and yearly fees, and some also offer daily and weekly options. Prices range from 500₪ ($150) to 3,000₪ ($850) a month, and more for a private office. Prices vary according to location, owner of the property (municipality-owned vs. private owner), office size and facilities.

See **Spaces** page **76**

essentials

Insurance

Israel has a highly progressive insurance system. All Israeli residents aged eighteen or older must, by law, be covered by the National Insurance Institute and pay national and health insurance contributions. On top of that, a high percentage of the population holds private health insurance and life insurance. Since 2015, private health insurance policies must have a layer of basic coverage, and private insurers may add more layers. The same idea applies to property insurance policies. Also mandatory is vehicle insurance: every vehicle must have basic accident and injury insurance. As for pension savings, these are required by law. Most of the population's pension savings are held with the private insurers, which therefore enjoy a constant inflow of deposits.

See **Insurance Companies** page **200**

Visas and Work Permits

To start with, consider arriving as a tourist. You'll need a passport that is valid for at least six months from the date of your arrival, which will allow you to stay for up to three months. After you feel the vibe of the city and check out the innovation scene, it will be easier for you to make your decisions about moving there. To take up employment, you require both a work permit and a work visa. To obtain these documents, you must submit an application for a work permit with the Israeli Ministry of Economy and Industry. With the work permit, you can apply for a visa recommendation from the Office of the Population Registrar at the Ministry of Interior. After that, you can start the visa application at the nearest Israeli mission. A work visa usually enables you to live in Israel for up to five years. Your dependent family members normally get a secondary visa for the duration of your stay, but such visas do not include a work permit.

See **Important Government Offices** page **200**

Taxes

The corporate tax rate in Israel is currently 24 percent, but it will be decreased to 23 percent in 2018. Every company in Israel must maintain bookkeeping according to the requirements of the Income Tax and Value-added Tax (VAT) authorities, and is required to submit to the tax authorities periodic VAT returns in accordance with its transaction turnover. Companies are required to make advance payments of income tax on account of its expected tax liability (as stipulated by the Income Tax Authority). There are four periodic statements that must be submitted: A submission of financial statements to the Income Tax Authority, a submission of Form 6111 (detailing the items of the financial statements), a Reporting Form 126 (detailing annual salaries paid to its employees and income tax deducted from those salaries), and a submission of an Annual Return to the Registrar of Companies. In order to follow the tax law properly, consider working with a local expert that is familiar with the Israeli tax laws, such as SZ Shvarts Zedkia.

See **Accountants** page **199**

essentials

Starting a Company

Establishing a company in Israel is a fairly simple matter according to Nadler Elishar & Co. The process takes only a few days. You will require an Israeli lawyer to notarize the documents you need to file (preferably a lawyer well versed in dealing with startup companies and other early-stage ventures). If you have cofounders, make sure you have a founder's agreement in place for a clear understanding of your rights, responsibilities and undertakings. The prospective shareholders and directors should sign the application form, the first articles of association and the first directors' declaration, and pay the standard application fee (currently 2,606₪, which is around $700). Before making any moves, it's advisable to have a chat and a coffee with a local law office.

See **Programs** page 58

Opening a Bank Account

Credit cards are widely used in Tel Aviv, and, generally speaking, you can use them to buy just about anything. Nevertheless, always carry some cash so you don't get stuck. ATM machines are everywhere and charge more-or-less similar fees, but avoid those located within local businesses, as the fees are usually higher. Since the local denomination is the shekel (₪), consider opening a local bank account to avoid paying high fees for currency conversions. To open a bank account, you'll need to bring your passport, visa and an initial deposit (100₪ is enough). To make the process quicker and establish better credit with your bank, bring recent statements from other bank accounts. Many banks will charge a monthly service fee.

See **Banks** page 199

Getting Around

Since the weather in Tel Aviv is mostly sunny, most residents enjoy walking to get around the city. The city's bike-sharing rental service, *Tel-o-Fun*, is a great option for touring the 120 km of bike trails, as it has a 24/7 service and two hundred stations around the city. Buses are the only public transportation option currently available inside the city, but a system of light rail is now under construction. Use the Moovit app to track times and buses, and remember that public transportation doesn't operate on *Shabbat*. If you prefer to use cabs to get around, download the Gett app. It's the easiest way to catch a ride and helps you avoid being overcharged by local cab drivers, which can happen to foreigners. According to Israeli law, only professional drivers are allowed to drive other people. Therefore, ridesharing apps such as Uber are not very common.

essentials

Telephone Contracts

With about 3 million smartphones sold every year (for a population of about 8 million), Israelis sure love to be connected. The larger carriers are Cellcom, Pelephone, Orange, HOT Mobile, Golan Telecom, Rami Levy and 012 Mobile. All offer discounted packages, which usually include a local SIM card, high-speed data, local texting and unlimited international talk for $10–15 per month. Make sure your smartphone is compatible with the provider's network specifications, and that you read the small print on the contract. Since some of the contracts automatically renew on a monthly basis, and most carriers only provide activation processes in Hebrew, consider asking a local friend to assist you in that process.

Learning the Language

Hebrew (*Ivrit*) is one of the two official languages in Israel (the other being Arabic). It's a unique language with the earliest examples dating from the tenth century BCE. Hebrew is not considered an easy-to-learn language for English speakers, as it's read from right to left and uses a vowel system that appears as dots and lines, which are added to words to provide vowel sounds. The more traditional way to learn the language is at an *Ulpan*, a school for the intensive study of Hebrew (from the word meaning "studio"). It's an initiative that was started by the Jewish Agency back in 1949 as a method to rapidly teach Hebrew to the multitude of new immigrants. Some other schools to consider are Berliz and Ulpanor, or local options like CitizenCafeTLV, ThisIsNotAnUlpan and Ulpanoya.

See **Language Schools** page **200**

Meeting People

Israelis are very open, which makes it easy to start a conversation and make new friends. Sports fans can join ball games, run on the beach or practice yoga on the Yarkon Park grasslands. If you love food and bargains, the flea market, the Carmel market and the Levinsky Street area are packed with people who share these passions. And, of course, going for a drink in one of the city's approximately two thousand cafes and bars will probably help you connect with others and meet new people. On the virtual space, join the SecretTelAviv group on Facebook to find like-minded English speakers living in the city. You will find dozens of events a week on websites like Meetup.com and Eventbrite.com, where you can hear great speakers. These events usually offer snacks and networking opportunities, and are a perfect way to make new friends while learning new skills.

See **Startup Events** page **201**

ups

Airobotics **32**

Argus Cyber Security **34**

Biocatch **36**

drupe **38**

Engie **40**

Feelter **42**

Hargol FoodTech **44**

HT BioImaging **46**

Lemonade **48**

Nexar **50**

prooV **52**

Ripples **54**

Zest **56**

startups

Airobotics

[Name]

[Elevator Pitch] *"We have the first fully automated, industrial-grade drone platform certified to fly without a human operator."*

[The Story] Airobotics dates back several years to when CEO and cofounder Ran Krauss visited his local electronics shop to get a juicer and was distracted by the drones on display. He abandoned the juicer for his first drone, and was instantly hooked. However, he wasn't content to just fly drones as a hobby; he decided to come up with a more industrial-grade solution for business purposes. He founded Airobotics with Meir Kliner in 2014. The company has since developed Optimus (an 8 kg drone capable of carrying a 1 kg payload) and the Airbase, an impressive 2.5 m² docking station that allows a drone to swap batteries, download retrieved data, and even change payloads (e.g., cameras and sensory equipment) via an automated robotic arm. All of this is run via specialized Airobotics software that can predesign and dispatch missions in one click.

The whole operation was developed with full automation in mind, which takes the human element out of the equation. As marketing VP Efrat Fenigson says, "The biggest problem with scaling a drone business is the cost and the availability of the human operator as well as the precision of the results." Airobotics sells their "drone in a box" as a service, and conducts missions, such as mapping and surveying mine sites, or performing critical infrastructure inspections, security patrols and emergency response services.

[Funding History]

Seed

External

Airobotics started in 2015, closing round A funding of $6 million from a number of investors led by BlueRun Ventures. In 2016, they closed a round B of $22.5 million led by CRV, and in 2017 they closed a round C of $32.5 million, led by BlueRun Ventures China.

[Milestones]
- Establishing the company in December 2014
- Preparing the first prototype in 2015
- Announcing round C funding in September 2017
- Receiving certification from the Civil Aviation Authority to fly drones without a pilot in April 2017

[Links] Web: airobotics.co.il Facebook: airoboticsUAV Twitter: @AiroboticsUAV Instagram: airoboticsuav

startups

Argus Cyber Security

[Elevator Pitch]

"We help automakers, tier-one suppliers, and fleet managers prevent, understand, and respond to automotive cyberattacks."

[The Story]

After over a decade of cyber security experience as captains in the Israel Defense Forces' cyber intelligence unit, Argus cofounders Ofer Ben-Noon, Yaron Galula and Oron Lavi, joined by serial entrepreneur and fourth cofounder Zohar Zisapel, sought to leverage their unique technical skills and create a company that could make a positive contribution to the world. They saw an opportunity in the hundreds of millions of connected cars due to be on the road in the next few years, and the urgent need to protect these vehicles from cyberattacks.

"Our mission is to keep passengers safe, increase public safety, prevent costly cyber recalls and maintain business continuity," says CEO Ben-Noon. "Argus helps customers integrate innovative and proprietary security methods, proven computer networking know-how, and a culture of cyber security vigilance throughout the design, production and lifespan of connected cars." Recognized by the *Wall Street Journal*, Inc. *Magazine* and *Fast Company* as a leading global technology company, Argus has a team of over seventy people, with offices in the major automotive centers of Detroit, Silicon Valley, Stuttgart and Tokyo. The company brings an arsenal of patents and tens of thousands of research hours to the fight for safety, security and privacy on public roads.

[Funding History]

Seed

External

Argus had its first funding round in September 2014, taking in $4 million. At the end of 2015 it had a $26 million round B funding, with funding from VCs and several other companies including Allianz, Magna and SoftBank Investments Japan.

[Milestones]

- Informing Zubie of a vulnerability in the Zubie Connected Car Service
- Raising $26 million in the series B funding round
- Opening the hood on the Argus multilayered, end-to-end solution portfolio
- Turning leading OEMs and tier-one companies into partners and customers

[Links] Web: argus-sec.com Facebook: argussec Twitter: @ArgusSec

Argus Cyber Security

startups

[Name] # Biocatch

[Elevator Pitch] *"Biocatch is a behavioral biometrics company. We provide banks, large financial institutions and e-commerce companies the option to do fraud mitigation and continuous authentication."*

[The Story] Biocatch was founded in 2011 by neural science research and machine-learning expert Avi Turgeman, who realized that fraud mitigation services might benefit from his research in behavioral biometrics. As a leading researcher working with army intelligence, Avi had extensive experience working to solve the problems of identifying what is real versus what is fake when it came to human behavior. The concept was proven by Biocatch's first client, a leading bank, although developing the product took time. "The technology was mature enough, but we had to vet the idea and make sure the product was solid," says VP of operations Dekel Shavit. "This took about a year or two. The tech was ready, but from a business perspective it was hard to create the space and convince the customer that this type of logic could work."

Biocatch tackles all types of fraud detection related to software by collecting and analyzing traits as diverse as the way a person handles their smartphone to the way they operate a computer keyboard. It uses machine learning to figure out a "cognitive signature" that can be linked to a person. Fraud detection using this method has proven extremely accurate. "The amount of false positives must be very low," says Dekel.

[Funding History]

Bootstrap   Seed   External

Biocatch was originally bootstrapped while it was creating its PoC and onboarded early customers. It then raised seed funding, followed by an A round as well as a bridge round.

[Milestones]
- Proving that our theory and technology actually worked in the real world
- Getting our first PoC with a bank customer
- Accidentally pulling down the site of a customer, leading to a redesign
- Catching fraud for a leading bank that no other system had caught

[Links] Web: biocatch.com Facebook: behvioral Twitter: @BioCatch

startups

[Name] # drupe

[Elevator Pitch] *"We rethink the mobile user experience with a new interface that revolves around people instead of apps."*

[The Story] Assaf Ziv and Barak Witkowski, cofounders of drupe and long-time friends, have had extensive experience as software managers in corporations and startups. In 2014, they joined forces to create the drupe app. Their idea was to reinvent the way users engage with their smartphones, to make the experience more people- and communication-based. "We wanted to address the issue of why apps, not people, are the first thing seen when a phone is turned on," Barak explains. With early support from Tel Aviv's Microsoft Venture Accelerator, their app was solid enough to get early funding from both Israel and abroad, and since then they've seen very rapid growth.

The app works as an overlay on your smartphone screen, with most frequently contacted people to the left and most-used communication apps to the right. With a single gesture, users can drag and drop (or "drupe") their contacts onto their preferred app (such as Skype, WhatsApp, Messenger and many more) and get communicating. It works for a range of other tasks such as making payments, scheduling meetings, pulling up navigation maps or making regular phone calls. In addition, drupe learns the user's habits over time, so that it can make suggestions as to the best way to reach a particular contact. It can even notify you of the person's whereabouts and give suggestions for the best time to reach them. Thus far, drupe has had over 15 million downloads and has received glowing reviews and awards on the Android app stores.

[Funding History]

Seed

In 2014, drupe closed a seed round for $1 million from Yigal Jacoby, TMT investments and Curious Minds. In 2015, they closed an A round for $3 million from Canaan Partners Israel and Sweet Capital, which boosted the launch of their product and helped them rapidly reach 1 million users.

[Milestones]
- Getting the separate rounds of funding, which were a huge boost
- Launching the app in 2015
- Reaching 15 million installs on the app store
- Being chosen by Google as one of 2016's best apps with an average rating of 4.6

[Links] Web: getdrupe.com Facebook: getdrupe Twitter: @getdrupe

drupe

startups

Engie

[Name]

[Elevator Pitch] *"Our app, Engie, connects to your car's computer and gives you updated information on your vehicle's diagnostics and fuel consumption. In the event of a vehicle malfunction, Engie will send real-time quotes from nearby mechanics directly to your phone."*

[The Story] Car technology has improved by leaps and bounds, but often there is a lot of mystery about what's going on under the hood, leaving customers at the mercy of mechanics and their expertise. Gal Aharon, who founded Engie in April 2014 with Alon Hendelman and Yarden Gross, explains how the idea of Engie formed. "We got tired of taking our car for repairs and not knowing what the problem was, let alone how much it should cost to repair and whether or not we were being ripped off." There can be a lack of trust in the mechanics working at the auto shop, even though most are doing an honest trade.

Engie has developed a Bluetooth device that plugs straight into the car's diagnostics system and uses dedicated software to inform you of anything wrong. This can range from engine malfunctions to battery condition or a host of other issues. All diagnostics are sent in easy-to-understand language. "Both my grandmother and I can understand the information," says Gal. Engie can also send the information directly to nearby registered mechanics, who will then contact you with a quote and offer times to bring your car in for service. The app also offers reviews of the mechanics and price comparisons. Forunately, the mechanics involved aren't put off by the customers' increased knowledge. Quite the contrary, says Gal: "A lot of them see it as a marketing platform, especially the smaller businesses."

[Funding History]

Seed

In 2016, Engie received $3.5 million in seed funding through an Ourcrowd campaign and was funded predominantly by Uri Levine and other investors. This enabled them to reach product-market fit in Israel and launch in global markets.

[Milestones]
- Launching in Israel
- Selling our first unit
- Repairing the first car with our service and receiving the affiliation fee
- Launching in the UK and realizing we had a solution for places other than just Israel

[Links] Web: engieapp.com Facebook: Engieapp Twitter: @Engieapp

Engie

startups

Feelter

[Name]

[Elevator Pitch] "We improve sales and consumer engagement in online shopping by providing highly curated social content on the web. We're a software platform with advanced algorithms that support consumer decisions and eliminate the need to leave an online retailer's site."

[The Story] In 2014, Smadar Landau wanted to buy a GoPro camera. What should have been a simple task ended up a time-consuming chore as she found herself spending hours scouring the web. Looking through the sites, she found only conflicting reviews telling her which model she should buy. Convinced there should be an easier way to make buying decisions, she created a new service: Feelter. Smadar recruited a team of experts to build a software platform that could offer honest reviews by pulling straight from social conversations. Chairman of the board David Chang says, "Instead of going to old review websites, people tend to use social media to make their feelings about a product known. So we mix social media reviews with traditional reviews. That's what's relevant for customers." Feelter quickly gained traction as a favorite among influential startup competitions. It won the 2014 Think & Drink competition as well as the 2016 G-Startup Worldwide competition.

Feelter works by filtering raw content from the web in real time, then performing a bulk sentiment-analysis of the data. "On top of that, we use AI to figure out if the people are talking about the exact same product," says David. Once that's done, an overall score for a product is produced, which can be integrated onto a retailer's website. Feelter is currently in the process of massive scaling in the US market.

[Funding History]

Bootstrap

Angel

Feelter bootstrapped in the early days and made preseed funding by winning influential startup contests, originally netting a $250,000 grand prize at Think & Drink to make an MVP. They raised an additional $1 million from angels and $3.5 million from two high net-worth individuals.

[Milestones]
- Proving the MVP – we had a great idea but needed to prove it worked
- Being accepted into MassChallenge Boston, an influential accelerator
- Winning the G-Startup World competition, which boosted the company's exposure
- Winning the attention of verticals by choosing the right verticals instead of trying to serve them all

[Links] Web: feelter.com Facebook: FeelterSystems Twitter: @feelterInc

startups

Hargol FoodTech

[Name]

[Elevator Pitch] *"We are the world's first commercial grasshopper farm."*

[The Story] Hargol FoodTech founder and CEO Dror Tamir has always been passionate about finding solutions for better nutrition. In his previous venture Plate My Meal, which addressed obesity prevention through promotion of better eating, he learned a lot about the general lack of protein in people's diets. The global demand for protein is expected to double by 2050, and existing sources (such as cow meat or plant-based protein) have their limitations. "As an entrepreneur, when you see a big problem, you start looking for a solution," Dror says, "and so I came up with the idea of farming grasshoppers, which are the most efficient protein source nature provides."

Grasshoppers contain 72 percent protein and are already in huge demand in countries like China and Mexico, with worldwide demand increasing. However, given that they are collected in the wild, there has been a limited seasonal supply. Dror and cofounders Chanan Aviv and Ben Friedman solved this by building the world's first commercial grasshopper farm. The vertical design with climate control has reduced egg-incubation time from forty weeks to about three, allowing for up to ten breeding cycles per year (compared with one per year in the wild). "We're turning seasonal farming into intensive farming," Dror says. Currently, Hargol provides whole grasshoppers for the worldwide culinary market and milled grasshoppers as a high-quality protein powder.

[Funding History]

Seed

Angel

In July 2016, the company raised $550,000 from the Trendlines Group (Israel) and Sirius Investment (Singapore). In July 2017, the company announced a seed round, raising $600,000 from Sirius Investment (Singapore) and SLJ Investment (Holland).

[Milestones]
- Starting our first grasshopper farm in Chanan Aviv's garage
- Raising our first investment from the Trendlines Group
- Establishing the world's first commercial grasshopper farm
- Winning eight international innovation competitions in twelve months

[Links] Web: hargol.com   Facebook: HargolFoodTech   Twitter: @HargolFoodTech   Instagram: hargol_foodtech

startups

[Name] # HT BioImaging

[Elevator Pitch] *"We're committed to saving the lives and improving the quality of life of cancer patients. We've developed an accurate, real-time, non-invasive, zero-risk medical imaging system for early detection and diagnosis of cancer and other pathologies."*

[The Story] HT Bioimaging founder Shani Toledano imagines a world where cancer mortality is only 5 percent, not 40 percent. This is a world where cancer is detected at a very early stage, and localized treatment can be given immediately. "I believe that vision can be realized only if the medical imaging systems are safe, available in clinics, and not as expensive as they are today," she says. A few years ago, Shani's father passed away from an invasive cancer that was detected only at late stage. The fact that it hadn't been detected earlier really bothered her, so she decided to use her engineering background to develop a new method of cancer detection. Shani didn't accept that the world should just settle for the same methods of detecting cancer that it has been using. "I decided that after losing my father, I would turn my pain and sadness into innovation."

She founded the company in 2015 with her partner Gidi Barak and called it HT Bioimaging after her father (Herzel Toledano). HT Bioimaging has developed a platform technology medical imaging method that detects the unique heat-flow characteristics of cancer and produces a processed image where cancerous tissue and normal tissue can be defined. Thus far, it can be used to detect and visualize a range of different cancers including prostate, colon, skin, lung, cervical, oral-nasal and more. They are currently preparing the 'first-in-human' clinical trial and developing a go-to-market scanner for cervical cancer.

[Funding History]

Bootstrap   Seed   Angel

HT Bioimaging began as self-funded but completed a preseed round in late 2015 with an angel investor, and another seed round in 2017 from angel investors. It also received help from the Israel Innovation Authority.

[Milestones]
- Completing our first pre-clinical trial
- Being one of the startup companies selected for support by the Israel Innovation Authority
- Completing the Med Tech accelerator
- Doing our first human clinical trials

[Links] Linkedin: HTBioImaging@linkedin.com

HT BioImaging

Lemonade

[Name]

[Elevator Pitch] *"We offer homeowners and renters full-stack insurance powered by AI and behavioral economics. We not only promise zero paperwork and instant everything, we're rewriting insurance as a social good, donating underwriting profits to nonprofit organizations."*

[The Story] When serial entrepreneurs Daniel Schreiber (formerly of Powermat) and Shai Wininger (formerly of Fiverr fame) were searching for the next big industry to disrupt, insurance was the clear choice. "The coolest thing about this industry is that it's boring and gray, so if you come into the market with a really fresh approach, you can rise above the rest," says Wininger. Like banks, insurance companies face heavy, complicated regulatory environments that often put off consumers. "There are a lot of studies about the most hated brands, and insurance came first, above dentists. For someone coming from the tech world, that's a huge opportunity to create something totally different."

"We're replacing bureaucracy. We aim to provide a full experience that has zero paperwork and is instantaneous." This means that users can get a full renters policy in less than a minute. Lemonade also puts a heavy emphasis on social good and is officially certified as a B Corp, donating all of their underwriting profits to nonprofit organizations. "We think like a tech company, and tech companies want to delight customers. We want to create the perfect experience so people stay with us." Lemonade is currently active in six US states and plans to expand nationwide throughout the year.

[Funding History]

Bootstrap   Seed   External

In order to be truly disruptive, Lemonade raised a $13 million seed round, much larger than an average seed round. The founders also raised a B-round of $34 million in summer 2016 to expand to new markets.

[Milestones]
- Raising $25 million in initial funding
- Hiring key people from the insurance industry
- Obtaining a license to operate as an insurance company
- Launching in New York

[Links] **Web:** lemonade.com **Facebook:** Lemonade **Twitter:** @Lemonade_Inc **Instagram:** lemonade_Inc

Lemonade

startups

[Name] # Nexar

[Elevator Pitch] *"With the mission of eliminating car collisions, we've built the first open vehicle-to-vehicle network that connects cars and alerts drivers of imminent collisions. Using the data we car-source from our network of vehicles, we provide data products for the automotive, municipal and insurance industries."*

[The Story] "If almost every driver had a ten second warning before a collision, we'd have much fewer collisions," says Nexar CEO Eran Shir. Eran and his former Yahoo! colleague Bruno Fernandez-Ruiz founded Nexar in early 2015, after deciding they wanted to drastically reduce the world's car accident rate. They developed the Nexar app, which turns a dashboard-mounted phone into an AI camera. The app works predominantly as a warning system for the driver, alerting the user to any imminent danger. Using machine vision, Nexar detects any number of endangering situations on the road ahead, such as a stationary car or someone driving erratically. When the app detects a potential collision ahead, it sounds off a loud warning beep, giving users a chance to take evasive action.

However, sometimes accidents are unavoidable, so Nexar also comes in handy for insurance reports. The app records video data and crash data, such as footage of another driver running a red light or speed at time of impact, which Nexar provides as an edited report and which you can use to back up your case. Nexar is pushing for as many drivers as possible to use the app in order for it to really reach its potential. The more that cars can start "talking to each other," the more peace of mind for drivers.

[Funding History]

Seed

External

Nexar has thus far closed two funding rounds. The first was a seed round of $4 million in 2015 that was led by Aleph VC. This was followed by an A round of $10.5 million in 2016, led by Mosaic Ventures and True Ventures.

[Milestones]
- Launching our first iOS dashcam application
- Making our vehicle-to-vehicle application go live
- Creating and launching the Android dashcam application
- Developing our ADAS (advanced driver assistance system) collision-avoidance alerts

[Links] Web: getnexar.com Facebook: getnexar Twitter: @getnexar Instagram: getnexar

Nexar

startups

[Name] # prooV

[Elevator Pitch] *"Our SaaS platform streamlines the entire proof-of-concept process. Startups and enterprises on prooV can open PoC opportunities for their technology needs, and test and evaluate hundreds of innovative software solutions by running PoCs on dedicated, secure, data-rich testing environments."*

[The Story] Cofounders Toby Olshanetsky and Alexey Sapozhnikov have been serial entrepreneurs for over twenty years in the enterprise software space, and have experienced firsthand the challenges of running PoCs with many enterprises. It was with this in mind that they decided to come up with a better solution for how to run PoCs, and so they founded prooV in 2015. However, they wanted to develop their platform from a broader perspective than just their own experiences of PoCs, so they interviewed over 160 C-level execs from around the world to gain a better understanding of the challenges that hindered others. The information obtained from those interviews helped to guide the development of the prooV platform.

The platform offers an end-to-end solution for running PoCs and enables enterprises to define the opportunities that correspond with their technology and innovation needs. For each opportunity they define, a dedicated cloud-based testing environment is generated and populated with data, APIs and servers to simulate the production environment as accurately as possible. It's crucial for enterprises to be able to test PoCs in an almost real-world environment to make accurate conclusions about performance, make educated decisions, and predict the future behavior of a solution before implementing it. With prooV, enterprises are able to do so in a very simple and secure manner.

[Funding History]

Bootstrap

External

After initially bootstrapping, prooV announced a series A funding round of $7 million from Mangrove Capital Partners and OurCrowd in 2016, and a series B funding round of $14 million in 2017 led by Helios Capital and Mangrove Capital Partners. OurCrowd and Cerca Partners joined the round.

[Milestones]
- Launching publicly in late 2016 after being in beta since the beginning of the year
- Launching V 2.0 in January 2017
- Having one hundred enterprises and five hundred startups on board by early 2017
- Taking our marketing, sales and go-to-market efforts to the next level by announcing series B funding in 2017

[Links] Web: proov.io Facebook: prooV.inc Twitter: @prooV_inc Instagram: proov_inc

startups

[Name] # Ripples

[Elevator Pitch] *"Our vision is to enable brands to reach their customers in a unique way that won't just bring a smile to their faces but will leave them smiling long after they finish their drink."*

[The Story] We now live in a world where we can send a real-time, personalized "tweet" or artistic graphic on a cup of coffee, and it's all thanks to the Ripple Maker, created by Ripples. The unit works in much the same way as inkjet printers except that it uses coffee extract as the ink and the foam as the canvas. As CEO Yossi Meshulam says, "We created Ripples as a marketing platform for the hospitality industry, so we started with foam-based beverages. This includes coffees, matcha and hot chocolate, but we're currently working on cocktails as well." The idea was dreamed up by two industrial designers, Eyal Eliav and Danny Lavie, in 2006, but they decided to put the idea on the back burner until the necessary technology had been created. When the technology caught up to their vision in 2014, they fired up the idea again, with Yossi joining the team.

The Ripple Maker unit is compact, wifi-enabled and fits easily on any cafe's counter. It instantly reproduces content (e.g., photos, quotes or personal messages) on customers' drinks via special Android touchscreens or consumer apps available on all platforms. The Ripple Maker is currently sold commercially to any company that wants to do real-time content marketing with a fun twist. Yossi says, "Our goal at Ripples is to put a smile on the face of the end drinker."

[Funding History]

Seed

Angel

Ripples was relaunched in February 2014 after an eight-year wait, with a seed-funding round led by Landa Ventures and angels. Since then, the company has had two funding rounds, both led by Landa Ventures, with Benhamou Global Ventures and angels' participation.

[Milestones]
- Launching our first product with Lufthansa
- Launching our second product and announcing our second-generation with other foam products
- Entering the Asian market
- The first large-scale use of Ripple-Maker on Celebrity Cruises

[Links] **Web:** drinkripples.com **Facebook:** drinkripple **Twitter:** @drinkripples **Instagram:** drinkripples

startups

Zest

[Name]

[Elevator Pitch] *"We're a new-tab feed of content suggested by marketers, for marketers. We decentralize professional content discovery by harnessing the power of the many. Our platform allows professionals from different verticals to suggest and filter content they believe other colleagues should consume."*

[The Story] With a wealth of experience in their respective fields of marketing and development, founders Yam Regev and Idan Yalovich had long been of the opinion that a key element was missing from the professional content-marketing world. "Before we created Zest, we felt that there was no effective, trusted way for professionals to consume valuable and relevant content," Yam says, "so we decided to start it as a weekend side-project to try and address this." However, their platform quickly gained traction and their growth exploded, so their weekend project began leaking into weekdays. Eventually they had to make a decision on whether to remain in their current jobs or move over to this "side-project" full time. "After we'd launched the product, we had a founders meeting and agreed that it was time to go all in," Yam says. The product became known as Zest, and they launched in early 2017.

Zest is a content feed where fellow marketers can suggest new content worthy of inclusion, and it's all manually curated and approved by real human moderators, something Zest makes a point of. "The only way to determine if a piece of content holds added value," Yam says, "is for other human professionals to actually read this content and make sure it's of the highest quality." While Zest lets the humans do the quality control, they use machine learning in their process to determine who the good content is most suitable for.

[Funding History]

Bootstrap

Zest is 100 percent bootstrapped and has been generating revenues from day one. They plan to be profitable by end of December 2017.

[Milestones]
- Officially launching Zest
- Signing our first paying client
- Being nominated as a finalist for Best Experience in the HotJar XAwards
- Crossing the ten thousand weekly active users mark

[Links] Web: zest.is Facebook: getzest.is Twitter: @ZestisApp

rams

8200 EISP 60
The Junction 62
KamaTech 64
MAOF Hybrid 66
Microsoft Accelerator Tel Aviv 68
SigmaLabs 70
TechForGood 72
Unistream 74

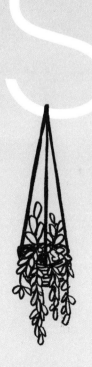

programs

- **Be an Israeli entrepreneur.**
  Your business must be registered in Israel.

- **Show exceptional entrepreneurial potential.**
  The program is competitive, so applicants should have a strong profile.

- **Have a good idea and a roadmap.**
  Applicants should not only have an idea for a product or service, but understand where they want to take their venture.

- **Have not raised more than $1 million.**
  Only early-stage ventures are considered.

- **Have a committed team.**
  Ideally teams have two or three founders that are 100 percent committed to the program.

[Name] # 8200 EISP

[Elevator Pitch] *"8200 EISP is a non-profit accelerator for early-stage startups from all industries. We offer five months of intensive, hands-on entrepreneurial training."*

[Sector] **Early-stage startups, all sectors**

[Description] The 8200 EISP Accelerator was Israel's first startup accelerator. Founded in 2010, the program has been at the forefront of shepherding the Israeli economy toward being a "startup nation." The accelerator operates on behalf of the 8200 Alumni Association, a non-profit organization established and managed by Unit 8200, the Israeli Intelligence Corps' cyber-intelligence department (the Israeli equivalent of the NSA). Each year, fifteen early-stage startup teams are handpicked for the program, which runs for five intensive months from February to July each year. The program is structured around overviews of startup business needs, including product-market fit, customer discovery, storytelling, business-model creation, growth and metrics. Teams also have bi-weekly sessions with diverse experts, including serial entrepreneurs, journalists and investors.

You don't have to be a graduate of Unit 8200 to get into the 8200 EISP accelerator, you just have to show exceptional entrepreneurial potential. The managing director Sharin Fisher says that one of the key differentiators for the accelerator's success is the ability to identify the potential of entrepreneurs in their early stages. "We believe that a strong team is the key for a successful startup. While business models might change along the way, the core team remains." This means that an important part of the screening process is dedicated to evaluation of the founding team members. "As 8200 alumni, we are big believers of 'it's all about the people,'" says Sharin.

The program has a proven track record, with alumni having raised a combined $450 million and employing more than five hundred people in Israel and around the world. Startups who participate receive free coworking space at WeWork around the world as well as access to a prominent alumni network. As the oldest accelerator in Israel, 8200 alumni form one of the strongest communities of influential early-stage entrepreneurs in Israel.

[Apply to] eisp.org.il

[Links] **Web:** eisp.org.il **Facebook:** eisp8200

programs

- Be a B2B startup.
  We accept B2B, B2G, or B2B2C companies, but this is not the place to validate a B2C company.

- Have a technical edge.
  We give priority to companies with deeptech know-how, and those who can differentiate themselves from existing technologies and become global leaders in their industries.

- Have a working MVP.
  Be ready to hit the ground running and participate in commercial pilots with partners.

- Have a 100 percent committed team with a full-time CTO.
  Every team member must be working full-time, and you must have a knowledgeable CTO.

[Name] # The Junction

[Elevator Pitch] *"The Junction is Israel's first commercial accelerator, owned and operated by F2 Capital, an early-stage venture capital fund. The Junction invests in and supports seed-stage, deep-technology startups that operate at the cross section of big data, AI, and connectivity."*

[Sector] **Big Data, AI, and connectivity**

[Description] The Junction is Israel's premier commercial accelerator, established in 2011 by investment professionals from Genesis Partners and F2 Capital. Focusing specifically on B2B deeptech (big data, AI, and connectivity), the program shepherds five startups through an intensive six-month program to help them reach global commercial viability. "We support companies with their business development and help them achieve traction," says general manager Mor Barak. "We're dedicated to supporting companies with closing strategic pilots and even paying customers, and to exposing them to the program's network of strategic multinational partners and sponsors." Partners of the Junction include giants like HP Tech Ventures, SAP, MunichRe, Enel, Deloitte, and Telstra, all of whom can provide serious networks and validation. The Junction also forms a major bridge for multinational companies to gain access to and support early-stage, innovative startups.

The Junction doesn't take equity but offers startups the option to accept a $100,000 convertible loan agreement with no cap from F2 Capital, which also looks to invest in their qualified seed round following the program's term. Startups can look forward to a tailored program (not based on a predefined syllabus), a workspace in the startup hub of Rothschild, and cloud-hosting credits, among other perks. With a vibrant alumni network and broad network of over six thousand entrepreneurs and investors, the program is extremely well connected in the deeptech space. "We can support companies in producing a product that can go to market from this very complex deep technology, and validate it while bringing the market to their doorstep," says Mor.

While some programs shy away from overt corporate partnerships, the Junction helps companies create win-win situations with industry partners. "Companies have the opportunity to drill down through their pilots and see the best go-to-market strategy through these collaborations, as well as to find strategic investors in the process," says Mor. Since its inception, more than 130 companies have gone through the process, and 72 have gone on to raise over $360 million, with three successful exits recorded thus far.

[Apply to] thejunction.co.il/apply

[Links] **Web:** thejunction.co.il **Facebook:** thejunction32 **Instagram:** thejunctionprogram

programs

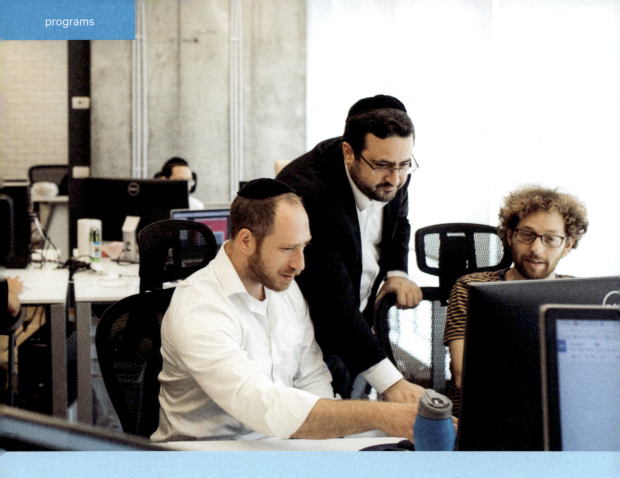

- **Resiliency**
  Entrepreneurs need to be able to weather the ups and downs of building a business.

- **Passion**
  While it is okay to come with no experience, you should have a passion for the field you want to enter.

- **Perseverance**
  It is important that applicants are willing to stick through the program and have determination to succeed.

- **A strong team**
  KamaTech is more focused on teams than ideas; they believe strong teams can do amazing things.

KamaTech

[Name]

[Elevator Pitch] *"KamaTech is a non-profit program with the goal of helping integrate Israel's minority workforce – especially Haredim – into the high-tech workforce and startup ecosystem."*

[Sector] Big Data, Security, Cloud, IoT, High Tech

[Description] Although Israel is a startup nation, some minority groups that are left behind in the startup ecosystem. KamaTech was established initially to help integrate the ultra-Orthodox Jewish community (Haredim) into the tech startup world, and has since expanded to include many minority groups isolated from the workforce. "Most startups are men who went to the best universities and were in the best units in the army, but many minorities and people on the peripheries of our society are not part of the Israeli startup nation," says cofounder Moshe Friedman, who himself comes from the Haredi community. Haredi currently comprise about 12 percent of the Israeli population, and their population is growing fast. Poverty is high within this group, as many have only a religious education, making it critical to integrate Haredi into the high-tech economy. "I myself got a religious education," says Moshe, "but I was very passionate about technology and innovation, and I started my own startup. I realized that I have a mission to help my community get education and opportunities to connect and succeed."

The program has grown tremendously since its establishment in 2013 in the religious city of Bnei Brak. "When we started we only had five applications," says Moshe. "Today we have a database of over 1,100 startups coming out of the ultra-Orthodox community." KamaTech teaches entrepreneurship and tech skills, and has industry cooperations with heavyweights like Microsoft and Cisco. "We have a special model where each startup finds a company to be like their big brother. We call it the Kangaroo Model. The company takes them under their sponsorship and give them mentorship, knowledge and office space." The Kangaroo Model has an impressive track record: on average, graduating companies raise $1 million and hire fifteen employees within a few months. KamaTech also offers a coworking space for Haredim and invests in minority-led startups through a VC fund.

[Apply to] info@kamatech.org.il

[Links] Website: kamatech.org.il Facebook: kamatech.coalition Twitter: @KamaTechOrg

programs

- Must have at least one cofounder who is Arab, Druze or Bedouin.
  This is a stipulation of the government subsidies allocated to the program.

- Must have a solid team.
  You must show that the team already has the necessary skills and knowledge to drive the project forward.

- Show that there is potential to enter the market quickly.
  We often start with founders that don't even have a company yet, so they must show that the idea is feasible, can be quickly developed and then introduced to the market.

- Must have an innovative idea.
  We want to see big enough ideas that will change the world or at least disrupt industries with technologies that weren't there before.

[Name] # MAOF Hybrid

[Elevator Pitch] *"We seek out untapped Arab talents, encourage them to run startups, integrate them with the industry mainstream, and actively engage them with the Tel Aviv ecosystem. MAOF Hybrid accelerator raises game changers and supports them in making daring ventures."*

[Sector] **All verticals considered**

[Description] The Hybrid program was created by the Ministry of Economy specifically to represent the Arab community in Israel, which makes up 20 percent of the population. The program organizers are very active in visiting universities and R&D centers across Israel to seek out Arab innovators who are developing unseen innovations in technology. A big part of Hybrid is to help the early stage ventures move beyond ideation stage and to fast track their ideas for market entry. They do this by first validating the product and then helping the startups to create a valuable network by introducing them to investors, accelerators and mentors. Hybrid has two bases (in Tel Aviv and Nazareth), but they're in contact with the Arab private sector all across Israel.

The six to ten companies accepted into Hybrid will take part in a seven-month program (May to November) and be given valuable advice and knowledge on entrepreneurship, strategy and business development. Each week of the program, the teams work closely with highly experienced mentors, all of whom are actively involved in Israel's technology sector. There will be pitch simulations, lectures and seminars, as well as tailored meetings and even the possibility of helping to recruit more founders to the team.

Aside from the considerable support the program offers, the startups will also get a wide range of additional benefits, including cloud packages from Amazon, Google or IBM; an intensive week focusing on growth at Google campus Tel Aviv; and an abundance of shared office space to use. There's also no lack of PR-oriented consultation to help get the brand message ready for targeted markets like Canada and the US. While Hybrid organizers are not shy about approaching those they feel are a good fit, teams and individuals are more than welcome to apply.

[Apply to] thehybrid.io/apply

[Links] **Web:** thehybrid.io **Facebook:** The.Hybrid.Accelerator

programs

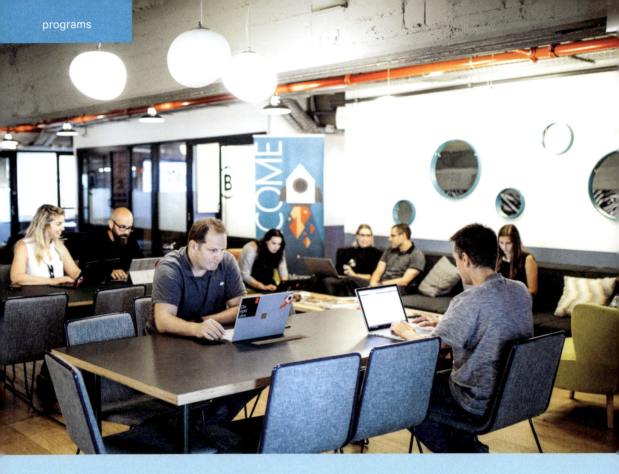

- **Make sure you're ready for help.**
  The Microsoft Accelerator only takes series A or series A-ready startups.

- **Have a solution for enterprise customers.**
  The program is focused on B2B companies, so if you're working on a B2C solution it might not be right for you.

- **Be ready to spend most of the time in Israel.**
  Either your CEO or CTO has to stay on-site for the majority of the sixteen-week program.

- **Be cloud-based.**
  The Accelerator is meant to encourage the next generation of cloud businesses, so your product has to engage with the cloud somehow.

- **Have a few clients to show.**
  Part of the application process will be showing that you've already achieved some traction with businesses. Make sure you have a few customers.

[Name] # Microsoft Accelerator Tel Aviv

[Elevator Pitch] *"We help startups to achieve more by providing them with the advantage of everything Microsoft has in its toolbox."*

[Sector] Tech, cloud computing

[Description] "A lot of companies have really good technology, and they're able to sell their products to a few customers, but they don't know how to scale it to something really big," says Navot Volk, who has headed the Microsoft Accelerator Tel Aviv for the last two and a half years. He's seen plenty of businesses develop great offerings, only to lose momentum when it's time to start expanding. "They can't ramp up their business. They know how to sell, but they can't do a copy-paste process on that."

Microsoft Accelerator exists to help startups that have the basics down and are ready move on to the next step. It takes round-A startups through a four-month program designed to prepare them for growth and give them the tools they'll need. It offers participating startups a program tailored to their needs, including CEO coaching and lessons on building a corporate culture, working with larger companies and recruiting the best talent. It also gives founders the opportunity to practice their pitch in front of real CEOs. In addition, Startups receive $500,000 worth of Microsoft Azure credit and individualized tech support to help them move their solution online. "We help startups to achieve more by providing them with the advantage of everything Microsoft has in its toolbox," says Navot. "Our help begins with a process called the 'maturity model,' which means calibrating the assistance we offer based on the maturity of the company and the maturity of the product. That's how we figure out what the weak spot is and how to use the right tools to address it."

What's perhaps most helpful is access to Microsoft's partners and customers. The Microsoft Accelerator program connects startups to B2B customers in need of their products. "If you're a B2B, there's a very high chance that your customers are also our customers. We can introduce you to relevant customers and companies using our contacts."

[Apply to] msatlv@microsoft.com or microsoftaccelerator.com

[Links] Web: microsoftaccelerator.com Facebook: MSATelAviv Twitter: @MSAccel Instagram: msaccel

programs

- **Have at least one technical cofounder.**
  Companies applying must be full-timers, with a CTO on board and the basic technical know-how to build their product already in place.

- **Have an innovative business idea.**
  SigmaLabs is open to all sectors, but your company should have a unique idea within your market.

- **Apply at the right time.**
  The accelerator is for pre-seed companies, so it's important not to be too early or too late. You should already be fully committed to growing your venture and have your basic team and an MVP/PoC/algorithm in place.

- **Show scalability beyond local markets.**
  Make sure your idea is scalable well beyond a local market and that it has broad potential to grow in your destination market.

- **Be ready for the commitment.**
  You should be prepared to work extremely hard for the next four months, to commit to working from the accelerator, and to be fully engaged with the program.

[Name] # SigmaLabs

[Elevator Pitch] *"SigmaLabs is a pro-bono accelerator, meaning we take no equity or fees. Companies receive deep mentoring, a technique we've developed that partners you with selected gurus and mentors over a four-month program."*

[Sector] Pre-seed, tech, all sectors

[Description] Only four to six companies at a time are accepted into SigmaLabs' "for founders, by founders" accelerator, a pro-bono program that takes neither equity nor fees from startups. Three times a year, companies that pass the interview stage undergo a deep-mentoring process that was developed to focus extensively on product and market fit. In this process, each startup gets a personal mentor who is not only a successful entrepreneur but also has access to the other mentors in residence. "They don't get just general, ad-hoc, one-time mentoring," says Tair Kowalsky, SigmaLabs general manager, "but someone is going through the entire process with them. We go deep into the venture's product and market fit, validation, tech, KPIs, marketing, growth and more."

Deep mentoring has paid off for SigmaLabs alumni, and most of their graduated startups secure funding within six months. They have a 90 percent funding success rate after less than two years of operating. "One more secret spice added by the program besides the deep mentoring is the fact that the accelerator team is very much involved in the venture, the biz-dev and the entrepreneur's life,' says Tair. "Sometimes just having someone ask, 'What's your challenge now? What do you need?' can have a significant benefit, as any alumni can testify."

SigmaLabs helps teams set their KPIs to reach their full potential and is actively involved in helping companies network and connect with potential design partners and other important contacts. Along with their "personal guru" and teams of engaged mentors, the startups attend handpicked practical workshops, receive office space and gain access to seed funds and angels, as well as to marketing, legal and financial consultation. In addition, there are a number of free business perks and the chance to form close relationships with the program partners, including Entree Capital, Yahoo TLV, AWS and Amazon, and Leumi Card. Applications are open every three months to companies that are tech ventures with strong full-time teams.

[Apply to] sigmalabs.co

[Links] **Web:** sigmalabs.co **Facebook:** SigmaLabsAccelerator **Instagram:** sigmalabsaccelerator

programs

- **Have an innovative technology.**
  We're looking for creative ideas that tackle the issue by leveraging the unique attribute that technology offers.

- **Demonstrate potential for large-scale markets.**
  We're looking for startups that can create global change and are addressing issues concerning diverse populations and geographies.

- **Have a GREAT team.**
  We're looking for talented, passion-driven individuals who can deliver, and for teams who cover all the bases.

- **Be passionate and driven.**
  Establishing and managing a double-bottom-line company requires true commitment and intentionality. We're looking for entrepreneurs who have the fire in their eyes.

- **Be at the PoC stage or post seed.**
  Your product or service should have been developed far enough already so we can really help you take it to the next level.

TechForGood

[Name]

[Elevator Pitch] *"Our mission is to create a global ecosystem that will support social-tech startups: those that use technology to address social and environmental challenges, alongside generating high financial profits."*

[Sector] **Social tech**

[Description] The TechForGood program aims to establish the world's leading social-tech network. It was set up to address the world's greatest social challenges through innovative technological solutions as well to offer great opportunities for startups who wish to make a large-scale impact with high revenue. TechForGood provides the entrepreneurs taking on these challenges with the professional support, know-how and valuable networking they need to grow and succeed.

The organizers are seeking companies that have completed first seed funding and can show either proof of concept or even a working prototype. Applications are accepted throughout the year. The organizers will initially have an informal coffee and a chat with prospective startups followed by a meeting in front of a panel of expert judges to determine who will be admitted to the program. Once selected, the startups receive their own office space to use as a base of operations and are assisted in setting out a goal-driven map to guide them in making professional and strategic decisions.

TechForGood opens the gate to the impact-investment world, and this includes providing access to impact investors as well as opportunities for exposure and partnerships. The program digs deep into how to structure an impact model and how to use the language of impact investors. Participating startups will begin to develop the DNA of a double-bottom-line organization and embed their impact goals into their business model. Additionally, they will be able to collaborate with TechForGood-affiliated corporations on their innovation strategy and development of their products and services. This benefits the startups not only financially but also in terms of creating positive social value. The Israel Innovation Authority has also chosen TechForGood as one of its landing pads in an initiative to bring foreign startups into the country's vibrant ecosystem under the Innovation Visa.

[Apply to] techforgood.co/israel/apply

[Links] **Web:** techforgood.co **Facebook:** techforgood

programs

- Be a high school student.
  You'll be part of the project from joining age at fourteen until you have a successful career and come back as a mentor.

- Have high motivation and a desire to learn.
  If you're hungry, ambitious, and want to work to develop your potential, this project is for you. Be someone who is looking to shoot for the stars.

- Be willing to commit to five days a week during the school year.
  It's important to make a commitment to yourself and your startup team. Once you graduate high school, your commitment fits your schedule.

- Invest in and give back to the community.
  The aim is to create positive social change in your home community through social entrepreneurship ventures. Your goal is to become a successful and relatable role model for the next generation.

[Name] # Unistream

[Elevator Pitch] *"Unistream aims to close Israel's socio-economic gaps by forging Israel's next generation of socially conscious entrepreneurs. Our entrepreneurship centers are high-tech hubs that provide a stimulating environment to establish and manage fully functioning start-up companies."*

[Sector] Technology

[Description] Unistream, a non-profit organization founded in 2001, is a unique program that aims to close the economic gaps in Israel and, in doing so, generate positive social changes. Unistream empowers youth and young adults from underprivileged communities to build and run their own startups and become social entrepreneurs. The program, which takes place in over fifty locations around Israel, is conducted over a three-year period that starts when the participants are still teenagers in middle school and continues into their early adult life. As part of the program, the teenagers are guided through every stage in order to secure their financial independence and the confidence to start building their career. Unistream aims for participants to receive the tools, knowledge and ability to dream big, ultimately enabling them to be a successful part of Israel's startup ecosystem.

Over 3,500 business volunteers from every business sector, spanning small business to larger corporations, take part in mentoring, delivering lectures, and providing valuable business connections. Under the guidance of these volunteers, participants are encouraged to decide on the core area of technology they'll focus on. They then execute every step in the creation of a startup, just as real entrepreneurs do, while learning all aspects of business, innovation and leadership and putting these lessons into practice.

The skills developed and continuously nurtured during the program cover the entire spectrum of setting up and running a business – everything from entrepreneurship, pricing business plans and market research to developing prototypes and learning how to present to VCs. Unistream also aims to create a generation of social leaders by getting participants to develop a long-term social project so they can contribute towards their community's success as well as their own.

[Apply to] unistream.tandemwise.com/contacts/unistream_student_application

[Links] Web: unistream.co.il Facebook: unistream Instagram: unistream_

ces

AYEKA **78**
Google Campus Tel Aviv **82**
Merkspace **86**
Mindspace **90**
SOSA **94**
Spaces Oxygen **98**
WeWork **102**
WMN **106**

spaces

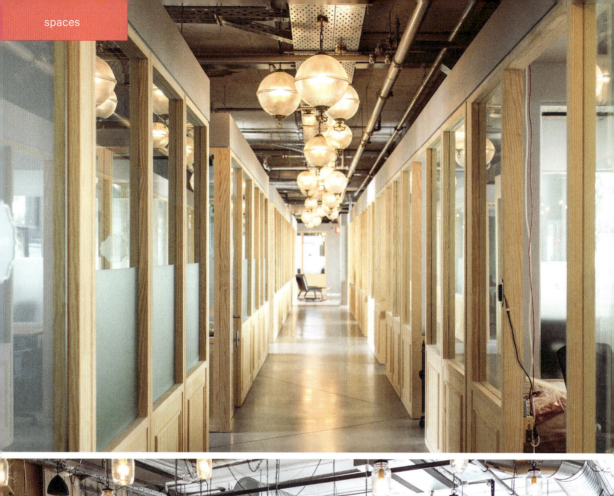

[Name] # AYEKA

[Address] 26 Ellifelet St., Tel Aviv-Yafo

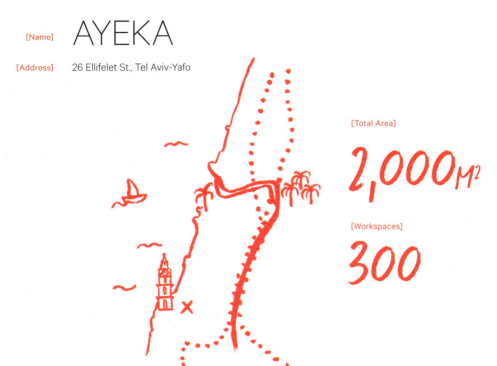

[Total Area] **2,000 M²**

[Workspaces] **300**

[The Story] Although AYEKA is not even a year old, it has quickly made a name for itself. Within six months of operation, it was named one of the five best coworking spaces in Tel Aviv. It's uniquely billed as a premium coworking space, and companies that pass the application process gain access to many luxury amenities, including a health bar, swimming pool, broadcasting studio and rooftop patio.

The founders have made a concerted effort to maintain a creative atmosphere that is a magnet for creativity and inspiration. "We try to keep the balance between both technology companies and other professions," says Daniel Chen, co-founder and CEO. "It's very important for us to create a mix of different types of people because we believe this creates a much better business environment." Startups sit next to artists, architects, writers and designers, and have access to a shared studio where they can create their own marketing campaigns in-house. Members also have the choice of using a salon area, private desk, private studio, or open common area. Setter Architects, the interior design firm who have created office digs for the likes of Google and Facebook, have designed a showstopping space that is nevertheless homey and comfortable. "The way the building is designed creates the feeling of a living room," says Daniel. "When people are here, they feel they are at home."

[Links] **Web:** ayeka.co **Facebook:** AYEKAisrael **Twitter:** @AYEKA_Israel

spaces

Face of the Space:

In 2006, Sharon Chen founded the first coworking space in Moshav Timorim, Southern Israel. Now she is the cofounder and CEO of AYEKA, where she follows her passion of connecting people and fostering relationships between businesses and individuals.

spaces

[Name] # Google Campus Tel Aviv

[Address] Electra Tower - 34th Floor, 98 Yigal Alon Street, Tel Aviv

[Total Area] **280 M²**

[Workspaces] **60**

[The Story] Google Campus Tel Aviv is more than a coworking space. Founded five years ago, the goal was to create a space that would become an integral part of the Tel Aviv startup community, connecting other players in the ecosystem with seminars, meetups and other programs. "From the start, one of the things on our mind was, 'How can we work with the community? How can we achieve something positive?'" says Yossi Matias, one of the campus' founders. "There were about a hundred incubators and accelerators already. We wanted to do something bigger."

Google Campus Tel Aviv isn't a traditional coworking space: there are no set memberships, and the workstations are only open on Sundays and Wednesdays. Instead, the campus tries to find new ways for startups to collaborate. These include Launchpad, which began as a two-week seminar that fostered new startups and offered them access to Google's resources. There are also programs focused on making the campus more diverse, like a Campus-created cooperation with Kamatech that works to bring Orthodox Jewish women into the tech world, and Campus for Moms, an entrepreneurship program for new mothers and fathers on parental leave. "When starting Campus Tel Aviv, one of the things I asked the team to prioritize was promoting diversity – to make it a place where we can see populations that are normally underrepresented in the Israeli tech world, like women, Orthodox Jews and Arabs."

[Links] **Web:** campus.co/tel-aviv **Facebook:** CampusTelAviv **Instagram:** campustelaviv

spaces

Face of the Space:

Yossi Matias is Google's vice president for engineering, with a focus on search and research. He's taught computer science at Tel Aviv and Stanford universities, and helped found Google Campus Tel Aviv to integrate the startup scene into the local community. "The principle is to have a place that is also a platform. Today more than ever, it's important for entrepreneurs and the community to meet up and exchange ideas."

spaces

[Name] # Merkspace

[Address] 121 Dvora HaNevi'a St., Tel Aviv-Yafo

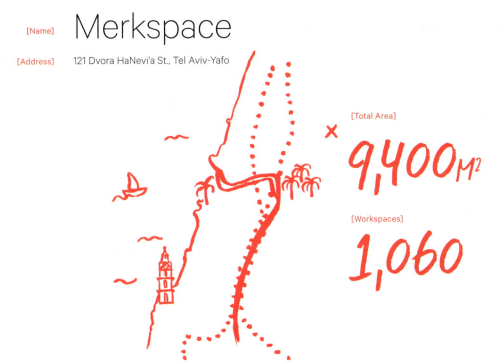

[Total Area] 9,400 M²

[Workspaces] 1,060

[The Story] Merkspace Atidim is part of an international chain of coworking spaces that originated in Tel Aviv. The space was founded in 2015 by Sapir Shpigel and her father Jacob Carl Shpigel out of a desire to support startup founders and connect them to mentors and investors. As Sapir explains, "We help companies grow, develop, raise funds, recruit, penetrate to new markets and acquire new customers. We're actively looking for business opportunities for our members (or 'Merkers,' as they're known) within our network." Merkspace has since expanded to three other locations in Tel Aviv as well as to Amsterdam, with more locations in the planning stage.

Merkspace Atidim is an ultramodern and relaxed setting with ample space for working in the private offices or among others in the open space. Atidim differs from the other Merkspaces in that it has one entire floor devoted to sports-tech innovations, and nothing gets the creative juices flowing for sports tech like an indoor mini football field and basketball court, both of which Atidim just happens to have. The Merkers are also very well catered for with less physically taxing social facilities: there's a pool table and VR games, a fully equipped kitchen with a range of drinks and snacks, multiple lounges and meeting rooms, and even a rooftop terrace for enjoying the free beer on offer.

[Links] Web: merkspace.com Facebook: merkspace Twitter: @MerkSpace Instagram: merkspace

spaces

Face of the Space:

Prior to creating Merkspace with her father, Sapir Shpigel founded a dating app with three friends during college. Initially, they were focused on building the technology for the app, but they soon realized that the business network, such as mentors and access to VCs and angels, was more important for a fledgling startup. It was this experience that led Sapir to create Merkspace.

spaces

[Name] # Mindspace

[Address] 54 Ahad Ha'Am St., Tel Aviv-Yafo

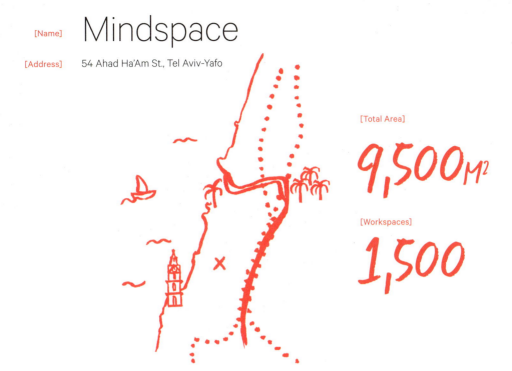

[Total Area] 9,500M²

[Workspaces] 1,500

[The Story] It's clear that Mindspace has found the secret to building a top coworking space. In just four years, the company has grown from a single floor to thirteen locations across the globe. "For me, Mindspace is much more than an office," says senior community manager Adi Klein. "It is a unique business environment that challenges typical workplace assumptions." Mindspace is a hub within the Tel Aviv ecosystem and is known for arranging a variety of workshops and events, including up to twenty meetups every month. "Mindspace positions itself at the center of the Tel Aviv innovation ecosystem," says Adi. "We cater to not only entrepreneurs and freelancers but also to innovation departments from the world's leading enterprises. The mix of companies of all sizes and from many diverse industries is what makes Mindspace magical."

Located on one of the most central streets in Tel Aviv, Mindspace provides a "plug and play" experience for its members. The all-inclusive contract includes 24/7 access, a fully equipped kitchen, and services such as cleaning and IT support. It offers private offices for teams as well as both hot and dedicated desks. "I'd describe us as unique, caring, entrepreneurial, professional and cosmopolitan," says Adi. It's no wonder that ecosystem heavyweights like Techstars Accelerator, Rise Tel Aviv (Barclays Bank) and other global brands call it home.

[Links] Web: mindspace.me Facebook: mindspace.me Twitter: @MindspaceME Instagram: mindspace.me

spaces

Face of the Space:

Mindspace Tel Aviv's senior community manager, Adi Klein, has more buddies than body cells. She's an IDC media and communications graduate and a world traveler, and when she's not networking in the Mindspace hallways or throwing professional events, you'll find her digging her toes deep into the sand of Israel's beaches.

spaces

[Name] # SOSA

[Address] 13 Shocken St., Tel Aviv-Yafo

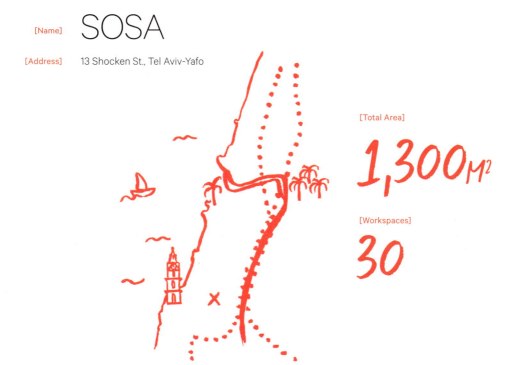

[Total Area] **1,300 M²**

[Workspaces] **30**

[The Story] SOSA (South of Salame) is located in a former industrial district and, in keeping with that vibe, the space has been given a beautiful industrial-chic upgrade. It was founded in 2014 by prominent Israeli investors and executives, including Chemi Peres, Rami Beracha, Gigi Levi, Adi Soffer Teeni and others. They wanted to curate different business interactions by getting tech startups, investors, VCs and MNCs together under the same roof, so they started an exclusive membership club offering mutual direct access between startups, investors and corporations. With all this high-powered business connectivity going on, SOSA provides plenty of space for mingling, including offices, meeting rooms, a fresh bar and ample lounges – and all in an open and welcoming atmosphere.

SOSA also has "corporate open innovation programs," which entail strategic partnerships with multinational companies, such as Siemens, Enel, Zurich Insurance and even the Australian government. "SOSA connects the supply of the startups with the demand from the markets, which creates business opportunities and delivers value beyond the space," says marketing director Gali Bloch Liran. "We're connecting the dots in the local ecosystem, and with our vast network and global strategic partnerships, we're also fostering a global network of tech innovation hubs." A SOSA space recently opened in Chelsea, New York, and there are plans to open another location in Tel Aviv.

[Links] Web: sosa.co Facebook: sosashocken13 Twitter: @SoSaTLV Instagram: sosa_global

spaces

Face of the Space:

Gali Bloch Liran leads all global SOSA marketing efforts for the Tel Aviv and NYC hubs. Previously she was marketing manager for the autonomous drone startup Percepto, director of strategy for Israel's Ministry of Finance in Washington, D.C., and director of marketing and business development for a retail company in Tbilisi, Georgia. She's also practiced law and worked as a flight attendant. She contributes to and thrives on SOSA's innovation energy.

spaces

[Name] # Spaces Oxygen

[Address] 62 Medinat Ha-yehudim St., Herzliya

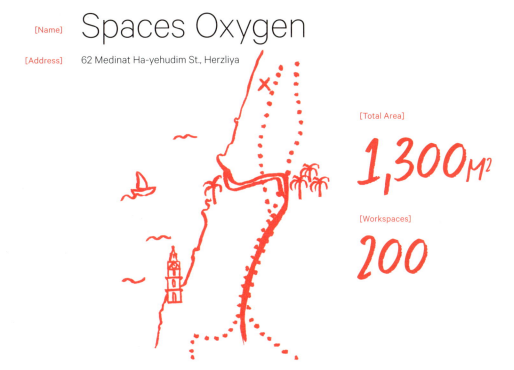

[Total Area] **1,300 M²**

[Workspaces] **200**

[The Story] Just north of Tel Aviv is a buzzing and creative high-tech district called Herzliya, which is home to Spaces Oxygen. Spaces is a worldwide network of coworking spaces that originated in Amsterdam. It began in 2008 as an informal and relaxed alternative to the more office-like environments of other coworking spaces. As community manager Naomi Green says, "You can wear a suit and tie if you want, but it's not obligatory. And don't worry about covering up your tattoos." Spaces also makes a point of offering flexible and tailored contracts to suit each individual tenant's needs.

Spaces Oxygen is set in a beautiful, refurbished building that offers a wide choice of different workspaces, ranging from more open-plan workspaces for entrepreneurs who like energetic collaboration to private offices for those who prefer some peace and quiet. Oxygen also nurtures a warm community feeling with regular seminars, meetups and movie/pizza nights. Startups that become members are well catered for with network access to patent-specialist law firms, mentorship from those who have done it already, and abundant cloud storage space. The space is complemented by an in-house cafe and a cute little outside garden with Wi-Fi and a smoking area. There's also a great selection of restaurants nearby, and the location is well connected to transport links.

[Links] Web: spacesworks.com/herzliya/oxygen Facebook: spacesworks Instagram: spacesworks

spaces

Face of the Space:

American-born Naomi Greenberg comes from a background in fitness and health management. As the community manager for Spaces Oxygen, she loves the challenge of implementing the vast range of activities that takes place at this coworking space. These range from informal movie evenings and ping-pong tournaments to the more professional tech conferences and seminars.

spaces

[Name] # WeWork

[Address] 7 HaPelech St., Tel Aviv-Yafo

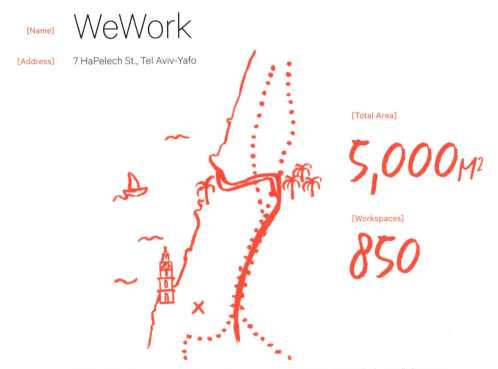

[Total Area] **5,000 M²**

[Workspaces] **850**

[The Story] WeWork, the juggernaut of future-of-work-style coworking, has pulled out all the stops in Tel Aviv. The space hosts four thousand members in three buildings, with a new building on the way to host another two thousand. WeWork also provides workspaces in an underserved area of South Tel Aviv that is more accessible to commuters but has a dearth of coworking spaces. WeWork serves every kind of coworking resident, from freelancers, startups and small businesses all the way to larger corporates, and it has perfected the art of providing flexible office needs: residents can expect everything from micro-roasted coffee to common areas, rooftop gardens, bike storage, craft beer, and access to WeWork's events and expansive global network. WeWork also negotiates partner rates for community services such as gym memberships, accounting software and health insurance.

More uniquely, the Tel Aviv location contains a first-of-its-kind hardware prototyping facility for community members who need to do rapid hardware prototyping. The lab offers 3D scanning, laser cutters, robotic arms, high-end 3D printing, and a metal, wood, and fabrics lab. "You can come into the space in the morning with an idea and come out with a physical product in your hand," says director Benjy Singer. WeWork also engages in social initiatives. It's partnered with Reut Group, which matches people with disabilities with makers of assistive technology, and donates office space to an NGO that gives scholarships to African refugees in Israel.

[Links] **Web:** wework.com/l/tel-aviv **Facebook:** WeWorkHaZeram **Twitter:** @WeWork **Instagram:** wework

spaces

Face of the Space:

Eilam Gazit, operation director for Europe and Israel, was one of the first directors of WeWork Europe and Israel in 2014, where his focus is on maintaining a world-class space experience for WeWork members. He grew up in a Kibbutz.

spaces

[Name] # WMN

[Address] 121 Dvora HaNevi'a St., Tel Aviv-Yafo

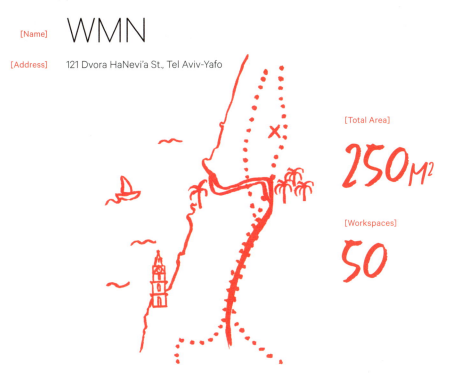

[Total Area] 250M²

[Workspaces] 50

[The Story] WMN is one of the most unique coworking spaces in the world. Within the startup ecosystem, only 5–7 percent of startups are led by women, but at WMN, 100 percent of the startups have at least one female cofounder. Founded by serial entrepreneur Merav Oren in 2015, this collaborative space emphasizes the needs of women-run businesses by creating a warm and helpful community. "It's a social initiative, not a business," says Merav. "It's a very special place: a true community initiative."

WMN directly tackles the lack of women role models and the low visibility of women in entrepreneurship, both of which can make aspiring female entrepreneurs lack the faith in themselves to execute their ideas. "They want to do something, but sometimes they're not sure they can do it," explains Merav. "So if they have an idea, we say, just come over, sit here and work at the same table as other founders just like you." WMN helps residents network and build bridges by connecting its members with other female founders, investors and executives from all over the world. It offers all the typical amenities of a coworking community along with subsidized space for female-led ventures. WMN hosts delegations from all around the globe and is a focal point for initiatives connecting female-led tech entrepreneurship. "If you're a woman at any cowork, you're one out of one thousand, but if you come here, you can really shine and reach your potential."

[Links] Web: wmn.co.il Facebook: WMN.COLLABSPACE

spaces

Face of the Space:

Merav Oren, founder of WMN, founded her first company (a sales and promotion agency) at twenty-six, and sold it when she was twenty-eight. Since then, she's been a serial entrepreneur. While working at a coworking space that felt like a "boy's club," she decided to open something with a different atmosphere.

Microsoft Israel 112
Gett 118
Bank Leumi 124
IATI 130
Reinhold Cohn Group 136
SZ Shvarts Zedkia 142

experts

Microsoft Israel / The Start Up Team

Microsoft's unique value for startups

"Microsoft's mission is to empower startups at every stage of their journey to achieve more," says Shira Fayans Birenbaum, Microsoft Israel's COO, CMO and executive management member. "Whether it's taking an idea from inspiration to working code, building a business through go-to-market programs or making connections with customers, Microsoft is there to help. By providing unprecedented access to top Microsoft resources and customers worldwide, powerful business connections, and industry expertise and technical knowledge, it is accelerating the success of countless startups in Israel and around the world."

Today, business needs are changing nearly as quickly as the tools available to companies, and it's essential to move quickly to keep up. Microsoft helps new companies do that, offering a suite of services that help startups meet customers' demands at every stage of their growth.

For startups focused on cloud or SaaS services, Microsoft's Azure is the world's largest public cloud platform, offering a mature and innovative technological foundation for any solution. Users have the technical help they need to get started and grow while utilizing a local team of dedicated architects and a global team of experts. Microsoft also offers its Azure customers business development and strategy advice, helping them reach new markets and customers, prepare legacy products for the cloud era, and fulfill local market compliance and regulation requirements.

"During the past few years, the industry has been shifting strongly towards cloud-based computing, and many tech companies are in the process of transforming their business and products to better serve their customers in the cloud era," says Coby Peled. "This creates new challenges everywhere you look: technology stacks and trends, modernizing code, DevOps and delivery methodology, business models, organizational changes and many more. Microsoft can help your company meet these challenges head-on."

If your company struggles with go-to-market hurdles, Microsoft has a variety of business and marketing plans built to open new doors through joint launch planning, global expansion, channel development, lead sharing and more. "It helps startups succeed at every stage of their lifecycle," says Einat Milstein. Yuval Chayo explains, "It helps by leveraging the Microsoft scale, customer base and channel access." Rachel Pekin adds, "As the use of Microsoft's technology grows, more Microsoft go-to-market benefits and services are unlocked." Microsoft can help you develop a targeted, consistent and positive marketing strategy to fuel growth, while the Microsoft Partner Network connects you to a global community of business development experts, including app creators, service providers and resellers – all working to add value.

experts

Most important tips for startups:

- **Offering cloud services:** Microsoft's Azure is the largest public cloud, and comes with extensive technical support. If your company is providing SaaS, Azure can provide the structure you'll need to get off the ground now and grow later.

- **Don't go it alone:** If your biggest problem is getting your company off the ground, Microsoft can help. Its go-to-market and extensive worldwide network within enterprise companies can help you design a business plan, launch your product and eventually expand into new markets.

- **A gateway into the cloud world:** Microsoft's StartHub can be one of the best ways to break into the cloud. It's one of the best places to meet Cloud Architects and acquire knowledge in Cloud applications and Cloud capabilities.

Microsoft Isralel / Tech and Cloud Computing

experts

Finally, for startups looking to get started, Microsoft operates StartHub (based in WeWork, 30 Ibn Gabirol, Tel Aviv). StartHub is both a venue and a virtual engine for startups, entrepreneurs and developers, giving them an opportunity to learn, evolve and make great things happen as a community. Any company has the opportunity to meet top architects and partners one-on-one, work on a variety of solutions and technologies in the cloud (including Azure IoT, Dynamics, Blockchain, security and cloud app development), and to participate in training programs and join meetups, hackathons and community events.

Mike Dickerson, CEO of ClickDimensions, is one of the founders who have benefited from working with Microsoft. "Microsoft's partner model has changed our thinking on how we choose core technologies. We've enjoyed great economic and technical support since our company's early days. Our CTO would tell you he's fortunate to have many technology providers now calling on him. However, the biggest challenge in building a successful startup is most often not the technology; it's scaling the sales and distribution. The ability to leverage Microsoft to get customers and to get into an established partner network has made Azure an easy choice for us. As an American CEO of a company with its technology soul in Tel Aviv, I've been amazed at the organized go-to-market rhythm we've developed with our Account Executive, our OCP team and even the executives in Tel Aviv. We have a repeatable, scalable way to connect with GTM [go-to-market] leads, partners and Microsoft sellers in geographies ranging from Brazil to South Africa to Singapore. We've closed more than thirty deals in the past twelve months that originated from Microsoft."

Issy Ben Shaul, CEO of Velostrata, has also worked firsthand with Microsoft in Israel. "One of the greatest challenges that a startup faces in its go-to-market, especially in the enterprise market, is access to customers. By forming a close and broad partnership with Microsoft Israel (as a gateway to global Microsoft) – starting from testing and certification, and continuing with introduction to customers and partners worldwide with the stamp of approval of Microsoft, all the way to coselling Velostrata with support throughout the sale cycle – Microsoft provides the essential glue that connects Velostrata with enterprise."

About

Microsoft (Nasdaq "MSFT" @microsoft) is the leading platform and productivity company for the mobile-first, cloud-first world. Its mission is to empower every person and every organization on the planet to achieve more.

[The team] **Shira Fayans Birenbaum**, Microsoft Israel COO, CMO and executive management member | **Coby Peled**, Azure Principle Solutions Specialist | **Yuval Chayo**, Partner Development Manager | **Einat Milshtein**, Partner Development Manager | **Rachel Pekin**, Commercial Partners Lead | **Orit Greenbaum Lipski** and **Ron Kaldes**, Marketing and Operations Managers of StartHub by Microsoft

[Links] Web: starthub.co.il Facebook: microsoftisrael

"The ability to leverage Microsoft to get customers and to get into an established partner network has made Azure an easy choice for us."

Mark Oun / Gett

CEO of Gett Israel

Mark Oun left the telecommunications industry six years ago to help build Gett's B2B business; eight months after joining, he became the CEO of Gett's Israel operation. In addition to his work with Gett, Mark is a mentor at Unistream, an organization dedicated to providing young people from Israel's periphery with the tools required to succeed in a startup.

Operating in a single market, especially one limited in size, is not enough for most companies. When you have a great product, you want to scale it as much as possible. However, scaling effectively is one of the biggest challenges every company faces. When you start to expand rapidly, you face new challenges and complexities. Issues that were minor in the past – for example, in org setup, in the tools and systems you use, or in informal processes – suddenly become much more important.

"It's not easy to scale your business by a factor of ten," says Mark. "First and foremost, you have to build a culture that enables you to get things done and move fast. Then, as the founder or CEO, you really have to know your customers, and know how to develop technology and products that are a great fit for them."

Mark says one of the biggest mistakes companies make is not focusing on their customers enough. To scale your offering effectively, you need to know exactly what existing customers like about your product so that you can build on those unique strengths and attributes. "You need to always think about your product and how it fits the market in which you operate. The product always has to be perfect for your customers."

You can make your job a little more manageable by shaping your company's culture as early as possible. If you hire employees who are independent and flexible, and if you manage to define and instill your company's values early, it will be a lot easier to rapidly expand while staying focused on the customer. "Hire people who can embrace change and be passionate about overcoming your challenges. They will support you when the going gets rough, and accelerate

experts

Most important tips for startups:

- **Know your stakeholders:** Look at what you offer from 360 degrees. In order to scale and become a larger player in your sector, you have to take into consideration not only your customers' and providers' business needs but also their cultural, financial and legal situations.

- **Respect the local environment:** When you grow, learn about the customers, operational norms and local culture in your new market.

- **Bring a benefit:** Have a clear USP, whether that's a technological advantage or something else that will make a significant contribution to your client's business or solve a problem they frequently have to contend with.

experts

the company's success. Also, be mentally prepared for change and for fast growth – envision it in your mind."

As an on-demand platform, Gett can help small companies grow. With its network of taxis and delivery services, Gett helps small- and medium-sized enterprises get their products where they need to be, and it connects logistics-focused companies with unmet demand. "We provide the infrastructure for taxi drivers to scale their business, helping them better utilize their time by matching them with riders who are as close as possible. Our Transportation and Delivery as a Service platforms enable companies and entrepreneurs to use their time as effectively as possible."

Gett serves both private and corporate clients; more than seven thousand global businesses – from local startups through multi-nationals – trust Gett for their employees' transport needs. Large corporations and small- and medium-sized enterprises all use Gett to ensure fast pick-up, quality drivers, and the ease and convenience that comes with managing all their travel needs under a single digital account. Gett inspires entrepreneurs by demonstrating that a smart platform solution can solve the challenges of both customers and providers.

The company recently acquired the Israeli app Streetsmart, which uses big-data analysis and artificial intelligence to map traffic routes and coordinate fleets of vehicles efficiently. Using the app, Gett picks up more passengers and gets them to their destinations faster, better serving its customers in over one hundred cities around the world.

About

Gett is a global ride-sharing app built on a simple idea: if you treat drivers better, they will treat riders better. Gett already has the best drivers in more than one hundred cities across the EU and US, and it is the global leader in corporate ground travel, trusted by over seven thousand leading corporations worldwide. Gett has raised $640 million in venture funding to date, and was selected by Forbes as one of the "top fifteen explosively growing companies."

[Links]   Web: gett.com/il   Facebook: gett   Twitter: @Gett   Instagram: gett_il

"You need to always think about your product. It has to always be perfect for your customers."

experts

Michal Kissos Hertzog / Bank Leumi

VP, Head of Innovation and Digital

As the head of innovation and digital, Michal Kissos Hertzog helps Bank Leumi navigate the challenges of disrupting the finance space. She's worked with a variety of startups to bring their solutions to Leumi's customers and knows a few reasons why some startups succeed and others don't.

"I get to work with many startups, and they're all unique and different," she explains. "But no matter the differences, all of them know the basic rules for success: make what people want and focus on growth. You can't be wrong regarding the first rule – you have to understand your users. It works best when the founder represents the user when trying to solve a problem he or she is familiar with from their own experience. The second rule is trickier, since it's subject to interpretation: how do you define the growth that is right for you? The key is to set your metrics carefully. Too often, metrics can go ignored, and founders aren't careful enough in deciding what factors to measure. The most common and unambiguous example is when companies measure an app's downloads versus its time of use and retention rate. It's not just about getting users on board - you need to keep them engaged."

Michal has a few insights regarding cooperation between fintech startups and traditional banks. First, if you're a fintech and hoping to collaborate with a bank or large organization, it's important for you to know who your best point of access is. Since different companies are organized in different ways, that could be any one of several positions. To narrow your search, look for employees with "innovation" in their LinkedIn profiles.

You should also approach a potential partner with a product, not just an idea – something that addresses a need their customers have. "It's okay to come with an idea if you're seeking advice or mentoring; otherwise, don't burn your pitch." Also, "It is usually unnecessary to elaborate to a potential partner about their business or their market. Talk about the pain point or the need you're helping to solve. Bring a demo and show the customer experience." Additionally, know the related regulations well. "I can't stress this point enough, as many entrepreneurs tend to neglect this issue."

Finally, partnership usually means implementing the fintech product or platform within the bank. Know that no matter how well you plan, implementation will be tough. You're going to run into unexpected obstacles, and you'll need resources to be able to stick it out until your business gets up and running.

experts

Bank Leumi / Finance

 Most important tips for startups:

- **Identify the problem.** It might be tempting to try to do everything at once, but the best startups start small and grow from there. Make sure you're focused on one problem you want to address, and that you've gotten that solution working before you start adding features.

- **Rinse and repeat.** Once you've built a product that solves a problem, iterate, iterate, iterate. Get it in front of customers to see what works and what needs to be changed.

- **Never set a goal you can't measure.** This sounds simple, but it is crucial for growth.

experts

Like other industries, the banking industry is undergoing an expedited evolution. Bank Leumi has been partnering with fintech startups to take advantage of those changes, and focuses on three vectors: (1) being part of the ecosystem and following market trends and technologies such as blockchain, artificial intelligence and IoT; (2) changing its own corporate culture so that it can be more flexible and able to adjust to future changes; and (3) partnering with fintech and implementing their solutions. "We're looking for synergies that will enable us to better serve our customers and offer them better value propositions," says Michal.

Working with Bank Leumi means getting your solution in front of millions of new customers. It also carries a certain cachet; the startups that work with the bank have had their solutions validated by one of the biggest names in finance in Israel. "It's not just about the scale but also about a seal of approval; they've proved their product to a company that has millions of customers."

Bank Leumi recently collaborated with two new fintech companies that offer customers new ways to manage their finances. First, a company called Paykey, a social payment solution that enables banks to provide their users with peer-to-peer payment options through any social media apps, such as WhatsApp and Facebook; second, a company called Nummularii, which is an investment advisory expert system that automates investment-advisory services. The two companies have had very different trajectories: Paykey needed around six months of work to go from its first demo to being implementation-ready, while Nummularii needed more design work before Bank Leumi began offering it to customers. What they have in common is offering a service that customers want. "Both are building their solutions incrementally, and neither one is afraid to collaborate with a large banking corporation."

About

Bank Leumi is one of the leading financial corporations in Israel, providing comprehensive banking services and holding approximately 30 percent of the domestic market share. Headquartered in Tel Aviv, Leumi has a presence in key financial centers across the globe, including London, New York, Palo Alto and Shanghai. Leumi is leading the way for innovation in global banking. Today, Leumi Digital spearheads the digital banking field in Israel, with a wide range of innovative services based on cutting-edge technologies. Leumi was the first financial organization in Israel, and one of only a few in the world to implement cloud-computing technology. Leumi is the first Israeli bank to launch a standalone, fully mobile banking platform, 'Pepper.'

[Contact] Email: michal.kissos@bankleumi.co.il

[Links] Web: leumi.co.il Facebook: LeumiDigital Twitter: @LeumiDigital

"The finance ecosystem is not a zero-sum game. There is an opportunity for everyone, and especially for more collaboration between players."

experts

Karin Mayer Rubinstein / Israel Advanced Technology Industries

CEO and president

Karin Mayer Rubinstein has been working with startups for years as a lawyer. She began her career as a senior partner and has worked as the managing director for business development at HFN, one of the leading commercial law firms in Israel, since 2008. In 2011, she founded the Israel Advanced Technology Industries (IATI), a private not-for-profit organization, as a way of bringing together the various industry organizations in Israel. Today, the organization's members include over seven hundred paying entities, ranging from VC firms to startups to R&D and innovation centers of multinational companies. As a seventh generation Tel Avivian from one of the city's founding families, Karin works hard to grow Israel's entrepreneurial ecosystem and ensure that the city is an international hub for innovation.

Israel is famous for its high-tech sector. It consistently ranks among the most innovative countries in the world and among those with the highest scientific output, and Israeli researchers are responsible for ten times the global average of scientific publications per capita. But that strength has its downsides: the country is economically dependent on its tech output, with the sector responsible for 50 percent of its industrial exports and 15 percent of its GDP. With tech playing such a huge role, threats to this sector should be taken seriously.

Karin Mayer Rubinstein has been working to strengthen the Israeli tech ecosystem for years, first as a lawyer and now as the CEO of IATI, Israel's umbrella organization representing all of the tech-focused industries in the country. IATI works to enhance and integrate the tech and startup ecosystem within Israel and to prepare the country for the challenges of the next decade.

One of IATI's goals is to grow the pool of engineering talent in the country. IATI wants to increase the number of advanced technology employees by 30 to 50 percent by the year 2020, and double it by 2025. "One of the biggest challenges the ecosystem faces is the shortage of engineers," Karin says. "Companies are looking for highly skilled employees, so on a national level we have to find solutions fast to address this shortage, and we have to make sure they can find the most talented employees."

experts

Most important tips for startups:

- **Addressing demand for engineers:** One of the threats to the Israeli tech sector is the demand for qualified employees. There are positions open and not enough engineers to fill them. IATI is initiating educational and training programs and working on both short-term and long-term strategies to influence government policy to address this shortfall.

- **It's all about the Benjamins:** Leading Israeli startups don't have too much trouble finding funding. The challenge is where it's coming from: most investment in the Israeli tech sector comes from abroad. IATI is taking steps to promote investments from domestic institutional investors.

- **The times are a-changing:** The tech sector thrives on disruption. To prepare for changes in the high-tech space, IATI is working to diversify the tech workforce, ensuring that companies are getting the widest possible pool of talent and perspectives.

experts

IATI has been approaching this goal in two ways: In the short term, together with the ministries of the economy and welfare and the innovation authority, it initiates training programs and competitions for young people interested in pursuing careers in STEM fields. In the long term, it hosts the Israeli Cyber Championship (and has for four years now). The event is a sort of coding Olympics for 400,000 children from 2,000 schools, and is cosponsored by the Ministry of Education and the Rashi Foundation. IATI also runs several programs to connect tech companies with the academic world, and it works intensively with the Israeli Ministry of Education to ensure that STEM topics are prioritized in the country's educational system.

The second big challenge IATI addresses is how to produce more domestic investment. In the first half of 2017, $2.3 billion were invested in Israel's high-tech sector; of that, however, only 4 percent came from Israeli investors. "Our challenge is to bring in more money – local money – to invest in startups," says Karin. "We're working closely with the Minister of Finance and the institutional investors [including the country's big insurance companies and pension funds], and we're working on regulations and education to try to understand how to get institutional investors to invest more in Israel."

IATI also works to increase diversity in Israel's tech scenes, prioritizing the integration of qualified women, Arabs, Orthodox Jews and other minorities, prioritizing adult human capital in the high-tech and life science ecosystem, and preparing the industry for constant disruption in the future.

"There's a lot of everything in Israel – multinationals, startups, incubators, accelerators. And there's room for everybody. But disruption is the name of the game, and no one will support you if you don't look five steps ahead. That's where we're trying to be."

About
IATI, the "Voice of the Industry," is Israel's umbrella organization of the high-tech, life science and other advanced technology industries, with hundreds of paying members from every level and aspect of the ecosystem, including from VC funds, R&D and innovation centers of multinational companies, startups, incubators and accelerators, academic institutions, service providers and more. Through this broad range of members, IATI connects Israel's tech ecosystem, provides solutions and support at all levels, and integrates the various sectors of the industry with strategic and ongoing governmental goals.

[Contact] Email: **karin@iati.co.il**

[Links] Web: **iati.co.il** Facebook: **IATIisrael** Twitter: **@IATI_Israel**

"Disruption is the name of the game, and no one will support you if you don't look five steps ahead. That's where we're trying to be."

experts

Ehud Hausman and Eran Bareket / Reinhold Cohn Group

Senior Partners, High Tech and Legal

Ehud Hausman is a patent attorney and lawyer with an MA in computer science. Eran Bareket has practiced intellectual property law, with a focus on life sciences and high tech, for more than twenty-five years, and is the cofounder of Gilat, Bareket & Co., the litigation and legal arm of Reinhold Cohn Group. At Reinhold Cohn Group, the leading intellectual property consulting group in Israel, they help new entrepreneurs and established businesses to maximize the capture, protection, maintenance and enforcement of their intellectual property in a way that's beneficial to their businesses.

Many new companies are started based on the potential of some new piece of technology or new application of existing technology, but valuable IP can be a blessing and a curse: for all the advantages it may give your company, you'll need to dedicate time and resources to making sure that your competitors don't steal your ideas in an attempt to replicate your success.

"Let's imagine that our startup is collaborating with a third party," says Eran. "The typical collaborative legal framework holds that each party retain ownership of whatever IP it had prior to collaborating. That said, we've seen several cases where parties entered into a joint research agreement only to realize later that the other party had been playing unfairly. They misappropriated information or unilaterally filed for new patents based on their partner's prior innovation. If you don't have a good IP portfolio at the beginning to address such unforeseen events, you're going to be worse off than if you had one."

Things get even worse if you find yourself feuding with a cofounder. Proving who created what when you're collaborating with another company is hard, but it pales in comparison to fighting with someone you've been working with.

That's why it's important not to delay sorting out your company's IP policy. Even if you don't yet feel compelled to patent your idea, doing so early can prove surprisingly beneficial: ten years down the road, you could find that your early patents establish clearer ownership of products you developed later on. And a founder's agreement can help you spell out exactly who owns what idea if you and your cofounders happen to part ways on perhaps not-so-amicable terms.

experts

 Most important tips for startups:

- **File for patents early:** You might think your tech is safe because you've kept it in-house, but once you begin working with another company or looking for funding, you'll have to share it. Make sure to secure your legal framework early on so you're not surprised later.

- **Get it in writing:** You and your cofounders may be best friends now, but who knows how you'll feel in five years. If your company is tech-focused, make sure it's clear who created what in case you ever have a falling out.

- **Make your IP part of your business strategy:** Your IP needs will vary depending on where your business is and where you want it to go. Having the right IP strategy can make your life easier at every stage, and even open up new opportunities.

Reinhold Cohn Group / Intellectual Property Consultants

experts

Reinhold Cohn Group helps founders straighten out their IP policies. With a combination of legal and technical expertise, its lawyers advise you on what you need to do to protect your idea and how to get the most value out of your IP once it's protected.

"I think that IP is inextricably linked to the enterprise's business goals," says Eran. "As IP consultants, we're typically involved in crafting IP strategy and making sure that the asset you're creating conforms to your dynamic business goals. We also provide advice when you receive threats from third parties, which – coincidentally or not – often come when you're trying to raise money. Suddenly you get a letter from a big player who's going to your potential customers saying you infringed upon their IP. We provide counsel on how to respond to these problems. We're technology specialists, and we bridge the gap between tech, law and business."

"In many cases, clients come with a specific predicament," says Ehud. "First, we see how we can address it, then we build a multi-layered strategy. We're strategy consultants, and we understand the business. We sit with the CEO, the CTO, the VP of business development and the principal engineers, and we create an IP roadmap with them. Once done, a connection is found at just about every juncture between where the business is going, the R&D efforts, and how the IP picture looks, so if another crisis or opportunity is encountered in the future, they'll be prepared and know how to respond immediately. We update this map periodically to maintain a strong connection between the IP and any changes in the business and R&D in the company."

About

Reinhold Cohn Group is the largest and earliest established intellectual property consulting firm in Israel. It offers expertise in filing, prosecution, renewals, protection, oppositions, opinions, due diligence, freedom to operate, enforcement, litigation, licensing, commercialization and evaluation, portfolio management and strategic counseling in all areas of intellectual property, including patents, trademarks, designs, copyright, open source, plant breeders' rights and trade secrets.

[Contact] Adi Yazdi-Danenberg: adyazdi@rcip.co.il

[Links] Web: rcip.co.il Facebook: reinholdcohngroup

Reinhold Cohn Group / Intellectual Property Consultants

"We're technology law specialists, and we bridge the gap between tech, law and business."

experts

Shlomi Zedkia, Ramy Shvarts and Galit Horovitz / SZ Shvarts Zedkia

CPA Partner, CPA Partner and Business Development Partner

Shlomi Zedkia and Ramy Shvarts are certified public accountants and financial advisers for international entities and startups, from day one to exit and beyond. They walk startups through all the financial and tax issues experienced by startups that are expanding globally. Galit Horovitz, business development partner, accompanies startups through their life cycle and assists in raising capital and preparing startups to approach investors.

"Being part of a startup is like being on a roller-coaster, with ups and downs and everything moving quickly," says Shlomi. Startups often have trouble knowing when they need to raise capital. In the worst-case scenario, an entrepreneur suddenly realizes that their company's money is quickly disappearing and that they need to come up with capital quickly or shut down their business. That kind of desperation can put your company in a position where it will have to give up significant equity, or even take on outside management.

"Planning, planning, planning is essential," says Ramy. "It's important to create a financial plan and use it as a guideline from day one. Know how much capital you need to get from one milestone to the other and how much time you need. You should be prepared to raise money six months in advance; it takes time to raise capital and find the right investor. Some of the most common questions we get are 'How do we value our company? How much do we need to raise? And what should we give the investor?'"

When your startup does not yet have customers or income and is still in the midst of developing its product, it can be difficult to value using traditional metrics. Instead, it can be helpful to approach the valuation problem from the opposite direction: How much do you need? How much do you need to get from one milestone to the next – from starting point to first users, for example – and how much equity are you willing to give for this money? That can lead to valuations that are a better balance between your needs and your company's appeal for investors.

Another problem that can come up when a company starts thinking about funding is that potential investors can ask for a lot of equity, and low interest can mean entrepreneurs have

experts

Most important tips for startups:

- **Plan ahead:** Think about when you'll need funding before you need it. Not having enough money can slow down your company's growth, and if you need to raise it at the last minute you might find yourself having to accept terms you aren't thrilled with.

- **Figure out what you need:** Knowing how to fundraise doesn't just mean knowing how to ask for money, it also means knowing how much to ask for. Think about what your company will actually need, and what you're willing to give in exchange.

- **Keep a long-term financial forecast:** To make sure you don't run out of money unexpectedly, try to figure out where your income and spending patterns will take you a few years out.

few alternatives. When this happens, we advise entrepreneurs to look for alternative investment options. That can mean raising a lower amount at first, then more once you can show traffic and user numbers; sometimes you'll find you have a lot more options once your solution has been validated on the market. Other options include government incentive plans and loans.

SZ Shvarts Zedkia accompanies entrepreneurs from day one, creating and maintaining their companies' financial foundations, and helping them to build their financial business models and spreadsheets to help make sure they're financially sustainable. When a firm is ready to think of the long term, SZ Shvarts Zedkia helps them create a five-year financial forecast, including market analysis and sector research. Through this process, the new company can predict how much capital it will need and when, and explore the kinds of investors that will best match its needs, whether that is VCs, strategic investors or passive investors.

"To get a higher valuation, you need to believe in yourself and your idea, be passionate about it, and organize your financials," says Galit. "Before you begin working on your startup, be prepared. Set milestones for yourself and know in advance when you'll need an investor. Together with the entrepreneur, we build an action plan that includes all the fundraising phases – how much money to raise and from what type of investor – all the way through the process and the negotiations. We prepare investor decks and match startups and investors, and we manage the financial activities and risks of the startup."

About

SZ Shvarts Zedkia is a dynamic and innovative accounting and financial consulting firm with offices in Israel, New York and Berlin. The firm provides audit, tax and financial consulting services to both the public and private sectors. Its professional team consists of certified and qualified auditors, lawyers and business development and tax consultants, all experts in their fields who can provide service of the highest standard.

[Contact] Email: galit@sh-ze.co.il

[Links] Web: sh-ze.co.il Facebook: shze.accountants

"Planning, planning, planning is essential. It's important to create a financial plan, and use it as a guideline from day one."

foun

ders

Fiverr
/ Micha Kaufman 150

Mellanox Technologies
/ Eyal Waldman 158

NFX Guild
/ Gigi Levy-Weiss 166

Oribi
/ Iris Shoor 174

StarTAU | TAU Ventures
/ Oren Simanian 182

TLV Partners
/ Rona Segev 190

Founders

Micha Kaufman

Founder and CEO / Fiverr

Micha Kaufman was born in a kibbutz to two Argentinian immigrants, whom he credits with his entrepreneurial drive. He worked as a patent and intellectual property lawyer for six years before starting his first company in 2003, and he's founded three more since. Fiverr, his fourth, began as an attempt to transform the way freelancers and customers work together.

What made you decide to found a company yourself, rather than work for an existing company?
As immigrants, my parents had to build a new life for themselves here. They spent the first few years in the country in a kibbutz, and when they decided to leave they were broke. That was how things worked back then, so when they left the kibbutz, they had to pave their own path basically from scratch. Seeing my parents' entrepreneurial journey influenced my thinking and approach.

Since I was a teenager, I remember thinking I'd probably become a businessman or an entrepreneur, but as I grew up I was still searching for the right path to get there. I thought graduating from law school and practicing law would be a good way to start that journey. The field I chose was very focused on technology, and all the clients I worked with were in the technology industry.

After practicing law for a few years, I felt I was ready to start my own entrepreneurial journey. In hindsight, I was very naive. I invested far too much time in things like setting up a company and not enough time learning how to market the product. Making these types of mistakes early in my career led to stronger foundations for my businesses later on.

What did your first company do?
My first company was a security software company. This was back in 2003, a couple of years after Google became a global phenomenon. We began by offering software to secure hard drives, and when flash drives became prevalent, we shifted our focus there.

Micha Kaufman / Fiverr

It was the early 2000s, the golden age of the shareware industry, and we put our software out there like many other software companies did. Before we knew it, our software started selling organically, and a few months later we found ourselves selling company licenses to organizations such as Merrill Lynch and Deloitte. I'm assuming they thought they were engaging with a company of thirty or forty people, but in reality there were only two of us. And this was not even our full-time gig.

If I knew then half of what I know now, I think the company would have gone further. But even with my lack of experience, the business made enough money for me to live off of and allowed me to invest in my future ventures, which was really the purpose. It also provided me with a ton of experience and important lessons on what mistakes to avoid in the future.

How has starting a company changed since then?

Today, I see twenty-year-olds starting companies with the knowledge that I only gained when I turned thirty or thirty-five. That's the impact of the knowledge revolution the internet brought, and that's what's so great about it.

That same revolution is also why a lot of companies you see today are pursuing poor ideas. With the barriers to entry so low, it's never been easier to start a company, and because of that many people jump into it too soon. People get into entrepreneurship too early on without any experience. You look at some success stories from first-timers who have done it, young people like Zuckerberg or the founders of Instagram, and you say, "Hey, if they've done it, I can do it too."

Fiverr is a company that breeds entrepreneurial spirit. It's part of our core values, and I absolutely want our team members to pursue their dreams. I also want them to take a measured approach to building their own future, and not rush it. When you work at a company like Fiverr, you're given the opportunity to experience what's it like to ride a rocket ship. You get to experience first-hand the dynamics of the crazy growth that comes from taking a company from a few people to tens and then hundreds of team members.

Can you tell me about what inspired Fiverr?

I was exposed to freelancing as an entrepreneur and hired many for my ventures over the years. In late 2009, we realized freelancing was taking a turn and beginning to grow at an accelerated pace. While it wasn't totally clear why this was suddenly happening, freelancing was already

"When I think about what makes a company successful, it's all about the people. Surround yourself with bright people who are passionate about what they do."

taking up a considerable size of the workforce. In the US, it was already 30 percent of the workforce, and today it's closer to 40 percent. This accelerated growth marked an opportunity for us.

We knew from our own experience that working with freelancers could be tough. The entire interaction is full of friction. It starts with finding a freelancer and continues with discussing and agreeing on the scope of the project, the deliverables, the schedule and the price. Although many industries have been disrupted by the internet, freelancing has largely remained old-school, and most of it – actually up to 97 percent – is still happening offline.

The idea for Fiverr was pretty simple. We didn't want to import the high-friction nature of offline freelancing to the online format. Instead, we wanted to find a way to use technology to improve the process. We chose to embrace e-commerce principles and make the experience of buying a digital service online as simple as buying a product on Amazon or eBay.

Unlike e-commerce, where products are standardized, services are very nuanced and subjective. The challenge we had was to productize services and bring to life a platform where ordering a website or logo design was as easy as ordering a pair of shoes. And that's exactly what we did. Today Fiverr is the world's largest catalog of services.

You said your first company was really naive. What are some of the biggest mistakes you made?
Early in my career, the biggest mistake I made was not being bold enough in taking risks. It happens to a lot of entrepreneurs. When you gain some success, your first instinct is to protect it. You feel you have something to lose, but really, when you're small and nimble, that's the best time to experiment and take bold risks.

In my earlier startups, I was not as growth-oriented or data-oriented as I now know I should have been. I made mistakes in not initially raising enough capital. I made mistakes by not investing enough in the best human capital, hiring the best and the brightest. The way I've structured and grown Fiverr is the sum of all lessons I learned from my earlier companies.

What's the one piece of advice you'd give to your younger self?
When I think about what really makes a company successful, it's all about the people. The one piece of advice I'd have told my younger self would be to invest more in surrounding myself with people who have deep passion for what they do. Your team is everything. They're the driving force behind your product, they're your culture, your co-pilots, your wingmen. Oh, and don't run out of money. Never, ever.

After you started Fiverr, how did it develop? What's its growth story?
Fiverr wasn't my first business, but I knew I wanted it to be my biggest. What I had realized from my past experiences founding other companies was that a really big idea should be able to grow organically without a ton of investment initially. The real root of Fiverr is its simplicity, and early on the concept was incredibly simple – just "What would you do for five dollars?"

Founders

Once we built the initial product, we didn't publicize it. We didn't take out ads, we didn't start putting out press releases. We simply let the marketplace and its underlying simplicity take off. It was so easy to create a gig that almost anyone would try it. After all, what was there to lose? That simplicity is what allowed us to build supply, which should absolutely come before driving any kind of demand.

I still remember when we ended up on the front page of Yahoo! News. Within minutes, the site had crashed. The traffic and interest was unbelievable, and millions of people were signing up and creating gigs. We truly blew up, becoming a global community overnight.

How do you standardize non-standard products, like Airbnb does with apartments and you do with freelancers?
This is one of the key differentiators of our marketplace, and it has everything to do with recognizing the particular pieces of a specific service. The broken-down elements of a blog writing service aren't going to be the same as a voice-over project, and when you have over 150 subcategories on a marketplace, it means you're going to be collecting a ton of data about each specific gig. We call it metadata, and it's what allows a Fiverr customer to quickly identify the perfect set of gigs for his or her needs.

Let's use voice-over as an example. Each prospective voice-over customer has a voice in mind for what they want. Is it male or female? English accent or American? Perhaps the project is narration, like an audiobook, or something like an answering machine.

Developing an understanding of each of these unique elements and building a marketplace that gathers all of that data is incredibly powerful. It allows Fiverr to more quickly get prospective customers to the service they want while also increasing the understanding we have about how these services are bought and sold. Freelancers are able to get customer interest and traction without prospecting for business, and customers are able to sort through huge quantities of services almost instantly.

[About]   Fiverr is the world's largest marketplace for creative and digital services, including graphic design, copywriting, voice-overs, and music and film editing. Fiverr's mission is to democratize lean entrepreneurship by giving entrepreneurs, freelancers, small businesses and even enterprises the resources they need to get things done quickly, flexibly and fearlessly so that they can thrive in the new economy. Fiverr's global community of freelancers have delivered tens of millions of high-quality gigs from over one hundred service categories across 190 countries.

[Links]   Web: fiverr.com Facebook: Fiverr Twitter: @fiverr Instagram: fiverr

Micha Kaufman / Fiverr

What are your top work essentials?
My phone and my laptop.

At what age did you found your company?
I was probably about thirty-one or thirty-two when I founded my first.

What's your most used app?
Gmail.

What's the most valuable piece of advice you've been given?
Take other people's advice lightly.

What's your greatest skill?
My curiosity and my ability to learn.

Founders

Eyal Waldman

Founder and CEO / Mellanox Technologies

Originally from Jerusalem, Eyal Waldman founded Mellanox Technologies in 1999 in Yokneam, a high-tech hub in the north known as Israel's "Startup Village." It's since grown to include a second office in California, and has become the country's leading supplier of Ethernet and InfiniBand connectivity solutions.

How did you get involved in the tech world?
I did my B.Sc. and M.Sc. at the Technion [Israel Institute of Technology]. The first degree I did was in computer engineering, then I went to work as a software programmer at one of the companies here in Haifa. After that I joined Technion again to do my master's degree in electrical engineering. I focused on multi-stage interconnected networks.

Then I started working at Intel, and after working there for three and a half years, I decided, Let's start our own company. After a period of time I joined Avigdor Willenze, and we started Galileo technology, the first company I was a founder of, in 1993. We went public in 1997 for $250 million, and it was sold to Marvell in 2000 for around $2.7 billion or something like that. I'd already left the company in 1999, just before it was sold, and a few weeks later I'd started Mellanox Technologies. It went public in 2007 for five-hundred-and-something million dollars. I'm still managing Mellanox, with a market cap today of $2.4 or $2.5 billion.

What motivated you to found your first startup rather than work at an existing company?
I thought that I could always work at a large company and be part of a big team. That's something that, if I'm not successful creating my own company, I can always come back to. But doing something myself as part of a small team was very appealing. It was very attractive to me to try to master not just the technology side but also the business side of starting a company, so I said, "Let's start doing that ourselves and see if we can do it rather than be part of a large organization."

What gave you the idea to start the company?
The first company, Galileo, I was one of the founders, but I wasn't the CEO. Marvell bought the project, and we worked with multiple companies in the US to fulfill a gap in system controllers and Ethernet switches that we'd identified. It was very successful.

From conceiving this company to building it, what happened? Can you walk me through its story?
We started as four guys in 1993 in a small incubator. We had a garage, just a small room, and then we moved into a house. We took about half a house for the company and started developing products. We had revenue about a year and a half after we started the first design, then we raised money and became profitable after about three and a half years, and went public in 1997 after four and a half years. So it was pretty successful.

Were you ever worried that the company wouldn't work?
That's always the case when you start a company: you always worry, and you always try to figure out what could go wrong, and that always makes you worry about whether the company will make it or not.

There was one event that stands out. We worked with a large company, and we gave them our design to review and see what we were doing. At some point we found out that they were using our idea in other products. That taught us a big lesson. It eventually turned out that they were only using it internally, but we were initially worried about them releasing a product similar to ours.

Why did you leave your first company?
We had differences of opinion, me and the CEO. Let's leave it at that.

I think it's very important to be aligned and understand there's always going to be disputes. There needs to be a process where people agree on how to decide those conflicts, and a hierarchy of decision-making. People need to collaborate and see things the same way when you're deciding how to make technical and business decisions. You need to be on the same place on the ethical curve. I think those things are very important – the ethics of a company, the structure, the bones of the company.

Eyal Waldman / Mellanox Technologies

"Everything depends on you, not on others, which is a great feeling of accomplishment, but also responsibility."

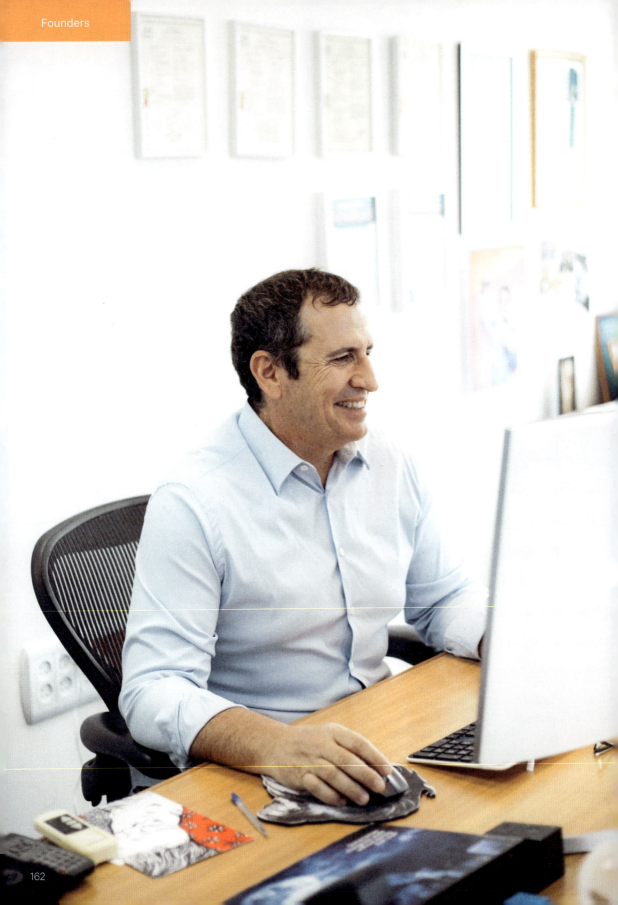

You also need to be aligned in terms of investing, in terms of the technical side and the business side and the operations side. So you need a lot of alignment between a lot of people.

You've founded two companies so far. Why did you found a second company after leaving your first?
In the first company I wasn't the CEO; I was VP of engineering. In the second company, I started the company and became the CEO. It was a completely different experience and responsibility. I wanted to see if I could do it myself and become the CEO, so that's what I tried doing more in the second company.

What do you like about the founder's lifestyle versus working for someone else?
I think you succeed or fail according to your own execution, not someone else's. Everything depends on you, not on others, which is a great feeling of accomplishment, but also a responsibility.

Is there anything you don't like?
I guess the stress. You have responsibility for everything.

From your time founding your own companies and observing others, what do you think leads startups to succeed or fail? What's most important?
I think it has a lot to do with the way the founders are built up, both mentally and in terms of their capabilities. It's also a matter of the markets and the technology advantages they have compared to other people. I think it's about building the team and raising the money, understanding what's important and less important.

When do you decide it's time to leave a company?
I actually believe in staying in the same company. I've been with Mellanox for eighteen years, and I was with Galileo for six and a half years, so I believe in long-term employment. I think people benefit more starting or staying with a company for a long time. It's much better than hopping between companies.

Founders

What are some of the biggest obstacles Mellanox faced?
We're going after very large markets, so the big obstacle is that we're competing with companies that are thirty or a hundred times larger than we are. You know, companies that have far more resources, capabilities, marketing power, muscle and so on. That's the most challenging thing, competing with companies that are a hundred times larger than you are.

How do you compete with a company larger than your own?
You run faster. You have to be faster, in terms of performance, features, schedules. We're usually an iteration and a half ahead of our competition.

What do you think about Tel Aviv as a city to found a company in?
I love Tel Aviv. I think it's a great place, and you have a lot of resources. The vibe is very fast-paced. Lots of technology-focused and international large and small companies are located there, so there's a lot of technological collaboration in Tel Aviv.

How has it changed?
I think it's getting better with time. There are more facilities for startups, there are more people who know what they're doing, so you can have better advisory boards, there are better funding mechanisms, and the VCs are getting better. Everything's getting better and better.

[About] Mellanox Technologies is a leading supplier of end-to-end Ethernet and InfiniBand intelligent interconnect solutions and services for servers, storage and hyper-converged infrastructure. Mellanox intelligent interconnect solutions increase data-center efficiency by providing the highest throughput and lowest latency, delivering data faster to applications and unlocking system performance.

[Links] Web: mellanox.com Facebook: MellanoxTech Twitter: @mellanoxtech Instagram: mellanox

Eyal Waldman / Mellanox Technologies

What are your top work essentials?
My phone.

At what age did you found your company?
I founded my first company at thirty-three.

What's your most used app?
Email.

What's the most valuable piece of advice you've been given?
Don't worry about things you cannot control.

What's your greatest skill?
Leadership.

Gigi Levy-Weiss

Founder and Managing Partner / NFX Guild

Gigi Levy-Weiss was an air force pilot before entering the startup world, and still credits his time in the military for some of his entrepreneurial instinct. He's been investing in Israeli companies for twelve years and is currently a managing partner at NFX, a VC firm that harnesses networks to help its companies grow.

How did you get into the entrepreneurial world?
Like everyone in Israel, when I left the military I thought I was smart enough to have my own startup. The first one wasn't very successful, but the second one was a little more successful. It got sold like seventeen years ago, and that got me into the tech world. I began working for the company that basically acquired my company. Over the years, I stayed involved in young startups, investing and helping companies get founded, and founding companies based on my ideas. So that's basically been my life as long as I can remember, being involved in tech and entrepreneurship.

Around two and a half years ago, I was meeting a bunch of friends in Silicon Valley and thinking about how I could make the Israeli ecosystem even better, and one thing that was apparent to me is that the link to Silicon Valley is really critical to many of the companies in the Israeli ecosystem. I started thinking about how I could be more involved in the ecosystem there and bring more Israeli companies into Silicon Valley, and I ended up setting up something called NFX, which stands for "network effects," with these two guys. We focus on network effects companies, and leverage our network of entrepreneurs, investors and mentors.

I thought most Israelis travel when they finish their military service. What made you want to found a company instead?
When you're an air force pilot, you leave the army much later. I left at twenty-six. When you leave at twenty-six, the idea of spending another year wandering around South America or Asia – it feels kind of late for that. You feel you've started your life a bit later. But why did I have the confidence to start a company? I think it's part of the Israeli culture. For better or for worse, in every Israeli company 90 percent of the employees think they'd be a better CEO than the CEO.

I was a pretty bad entrepreneur to start with, but I tried to learn fast. What the air force teaches you, which I really like, is that it doesn't matter how good you are to start with; it matters how

fast you learn. This is a principle the air force applies when selecting pilots. The system really doesn't care how good you are the minute you get in; it only looks at how you improve in a very short time. I've been trying to apply that to management, because I think it's very applicable. It's about how fast I can learn and how few mistakes I make twice.

What kinds of things do you look for in companies you invest in?
It varies, depending on the stage of the company. When you invest in a growth-stage company, you look at the team, but the numbers and business progress are the main thing. When you invest in an A-round company, you look at the team and the product-market fit and the growth trajectory. In seed, I sometimes look only at the team.

When people ask me what I look for, I usually say 70 percent team, 20 percent domain and only 10 percent idea. The idea is only 10 percent because I've never invested in a company that kept the same idea they started with all the way to the exit. There's always some kind of permutation and iteration. The domain is because there are domains that I don't invest in. Serving cellular operators, for example. I wouldn't do that today, because they're struggling. Anybody serving them is going to have a tough journey.

On the team, the one thing I look for more than anything else is speed. If there's one thing that I came to understand, it's that the main predictor of a team's ability to win is speed. It took me years to be able to describe it, until my partner in the Valley once gave me an analogy and I loved it. He said that for a startup, going up against the larger companies is like trying to win in chess against a grand master. I'm never going to win. But if somebody lets me play two turns for every turn the grand master takes, even I can win. That's exactly the startup world. As long as a startup moves dramatically faster than the larger companies, it stands a chance to win. The minute it slows down, that's the end of the game.

What are some of the things you've seen that cause startups to fail?
The definition of failure in a startup for me is running out of money before you find your product-market fit. Once you find your product-market fit, you're very likely to be able to raise money. So the question is, what makes these teams run out of money before finding their product-market fit?

"*As long as a startup moves dramatically faster than the larger companies, it stands a chance to win. The minute it slows down, that's the end of the game.*"

I've found a few things that are probably the main reasons. One is speed: when we invest in a company in NFX, we work with them on accelerating their speed. Once they move fast enough, we tell them they need to ask themselves every day if they're still fast enough. Every few months, we'd do something we called the Speed Boost. We'd invite companies, have them share best practices, and get them all to remember they can be faster.

The second thing I've seen is poor team communication. This is one of the topics that's least spoken about in the tech ecosystem. The founder relationships are among the top reasons companies fail. Some founders would call me "the psychologist" because they'd come to me with their domestic disputes. But what I tell the entrepreneurs I invest in is that, just like in a "real" relationship or marriage, if you're not open and you keep things deep inside, the relationship eventually explodes. So founders that want to build something great together have to be 100 percent open with each other. They have to lose their egos.

The third thing is when companies give up – often without being aware that they gave up – on their efforts to reach product-market fit. People end up tricking themselves because they don't want to look in the mirror and see the real picture. They lie to themselves and say that something's good enough, or it's going to get better, or it's improving when it's really not improving enough. They make small changes, but these aren't enough to find a product-market fit. They need big bold moves.

The last one is something that took me a few years to recognize. Some teams just don't have the skill to raise money. I used to think raising money was a tactical skill, something you just need to be able to do, but I've learned over the years it's not that anymore. Some people have that sales ability, and others don't, or not as much. The ones who have that raise more money, so they have more time to do more iterations and find that product-market fit. So when I see a team that doesn't have that fund-raising ability, that's a big red flag for me.

How has Tel Aviv evolved as an entrepreneurial ecosystem?

Tel Aviv has become the best ecosystem in the world for me. I've got this entire thesis about how Silicon Valley is the product of a network effect, with all the nodes and the density getting

Founders

to the point that it's so easy to start a startup. Tel Aviv is the second city to have this network effect at the same density. There's enough people here who understand tech and startups, including investors, service providers, coworking spaces, universities and everything. It's the second highest density after Silicon valley, which dramatically increases your chances of being able to set up a successful startup.

Then you've got the army, which is this great place for creating tech talent. Kids get to do things that no other kid in the world gets to do, working on these complex systems and complex problems in an amazingly professional environment. It's like a huge on-the-job startup university that adds new talent to the pool every year.

Then there's the unique thing about Israel, which is a bit similar to Silicon Valley: unlike in London or New York, tech is the top ecosystem. That's important. If the top ecosystem is financial services, top graduates are going to go into hedge funds before they go into tech. And you need these people. In Israel, we don't have financial services, we don't have natural resources – we don't have many of these since our local market is so small. So everybody who's really smart or really good goes into tech. That's the most desirable ecosystem and the one the top people go into, which makes it so phenomenal. On top of that there's the Israeli culture: the lack of fear of failure, and the understanding that with big risks come big rewards.

It all boils down to what I call the "mother test": What would your mother say is the best route for her kid to take career-wise? In Japan, they'd say go get a job at a large corporation to secure your future; but in Israel, they'd say go start a startup, because that's your way to social mobility.

[About]   NFX is an early-stage seed and A fund operating out of Silicon Valley and Israel. It focuses on top founders who are building network-effects businesses and helps them to harness the magic of network effects for their business to accelerate their growth.

[Links]   Web: nfx.com Facebook: nfxguild Twitter: @NFXGuild

What are your top work essentials?
My phone.

At what age did you found your company?
I was twenty-six when I founded my first.

What's your most used app?
It's gonna be very sad: email.

What's the most valuable piece of advice you've been given?
Someone once told me, "You'll only be successful if you remember that everyone you ever meet can teach you something you don't know."

What's your greatest skill?
I would like to think it's understanding people and what drives them.

Founders

Iris Shoor

CEO and Founder / Oribi

Iris Shoor founded her first company right out of university, and has built two more since. She's used her background in architecture to create products that change how companies visualize and interact with design and engineering problems. Her current company, Oribi, wants to make data analytics easy for anyone to access and utilize.

How did you get involved in the startup community?
I studied architecture, and when I graduated I decided I didn't want to be an architect. At that time, it seemed like everybody in Israel was founding a startup. For some reason it seemed like it was easy to raise money and build a company, and I decided that's the path I wanted to take. The first company I cofounded, VisualTao, was based on my background and focused on using cloud technology for designers and engineers.

It was our first company, and a lot of what we did was very clueless and naive. We decided to focus on architecture since I had a background in the subject. That may have been my first mistake. Instead of researching what was in demand or what had a market, we instead tried to do something that matched our backgrounds. We built technology that allowed people to use CAD files for 2D and 3D modeling on web and mobile devices, so instead of utilizing hardware-intense modeling programs, teams could use our software and modeling tools to simply edit drawings online using our mobile app. It took us a very long time to raise our funding at first, then everything started to get going. We were acquired by Autodesk in 2009, three and a half years after we founded the company.

Our biggest achievement was looking at a problem and creating a solution that people love. And the company is still doing well. Today there are over two hundred people who work on the product, and ten million users worldwide.

Could you describe Oribi?
After VisualTao was acquired, I spent the next two years working for Autodesk, then created another company called Takipi (later called OverOps) that helps engineers figure out where their code has problems.

Iris Shoor / Oribi

Then about a year and a half ago, I decided I wanted to start something new. When I decided I wanted to build a new company, I knew it would be a B2B company, but I hate enterprise sales and love wide-scale and simple products. I wanted to develop something that would address companies' analytics problems but also be really simple, something everyone could use. Everybody needs data, and people want to understand what drives their business, but today, all of the products are super expensive and require complex integration processes. Beyond that, they tend to require dedicated support staff, both to operate and to make the results useful. This creates a really frustrating user experience. I don't know any business intelligence tool that people actually love.

So what I decided to do with Oribi was create a new approach to data and analytics. We actually created a new type of analytics software, which is much easier to activate and install. You usually need to hire developers to insert some code into your app or your product in order to begin gathering useful data from it, but with Oribi you can immediately start tracking usage data without going through that. It tells you all the key factors about your software: who's using it, when, how, for what.

The other aspect of Oribi is creating a whole new product experience. So instead of showing lots of tables and data that require you to work hard to utilize what you've gathered, Oribi helps you interpret that data and presents it in a more useful way. The platform tells you what's new, what's interesting, what you should notice – and that's it. No tables, no endless data, no confusing presentation.

What's driven you to found so many companies of your own? Why not work at an established company?
I think we were in an environment where everyone around us was founding companies. It seemed like everyone in Tel Aviv at that time had founded a startup or was working for one, so it seemed like a natural thing to do.

Have you ever regretted that?
No, but it's been challenging. I think that the main challenge was probably the mental one. There were all the professional challenges of learning all the basics, figuring out the technical parts of our products and working out the business sides of the companies. But the biggest challenge has been not being able to tell if I'm crazy or I'm doing something right.

With my first company, for the first year and a half – until we raised the seed money – we were moving between feeling like we were totally crazy and making a huge mistake and feeling like everything is good and we're on top of the world. It's difficult to maintain perspective and keep focused on the problem in front of you. It was difficult to just continue doing what we were doing and not think we were completely crazy for doing it.

"What makes the Tel Aviv ecosystem special is how much other companies' people are willing to help each other."

What's been the hardest part of building the businesses?
I think the hardest part was with my previous startup. It was around raising money, which was always very challenging. When you're trying to get funding for a new company, you're trying to convince someone that what you're making is actually going to work, and that requires a little storytelling. I'm usually not about the story, though; what I like to focus on is all the smart parts of making a product really work and getting people to use it and love it, especially at the early stages where there's this basic product and you know it's going to work, and make something work a lot better and a lot more intuitively for customers. So it was difficult for me to change modes. I like working on the details of how a product works and how it can be improved, and I had to present a bigger-picture story of how the product could look and what need it could serve when all of that was done.

How did you address that?
I had to learn to present the product in a new way. I think that while I'm a big believer in creating simple and good products, it's also very important to create a good story. It was a very important process for me to build the vision and build the story behind the product to help our investors understand our goal, which was to create something that would help engineers and programmers work more effectively, and change how they interacted with their work.

When your first company was acquired by Autodesk, how did you know that it was the right time?
I didn't, but one thing that was important for us was to work with the right partner, one that would be best for the company. That immediately limited who we could work with; there aren't many larger companies with the technological capabilities to acquire companies that deal with 3D- and 2D-modeling and grow those features. That's kind of a good thing, because it limited our potential competition, but it also meant it was less likely that we'd be acquired at all. So when Autodesk acquired the company, I can't say it was the right timing, but I can say that it worked very well. It was the right partner.

Why did you want the company to be acquired at all? Why not keep running it yourself?
I think because it was my first company, and we got a good offer. We'd reached a point where we'd built it as far as we could ourselves. When we decided that it was going to succeed better if it was part of Autodesk, we decided to sell it.

But I don't think that's going to be the case with Oribi. I have more experience now and bigger goals. The difference in maturity makes you want to build a more significant

Founders

company. It's always tempting to sell your first startup, take the experience and move on. Now I'm building this company differently to become a bigger company and build a more significant product.

What do you like and dislike about being a founder?
What I love about the startup life is that everything changes very rapidly. Every year is completely different from the last year, with a constantly changing set of demands. At first I had to learn how to do product development, then how to do marketing and sales. Even today I'm struggling with lots of new challenges, like how to build a visual language for presenting data effectively.

So I feel constantly challenged. It's impossible to get into a comfort zone. There are some days I wish I could just come to work and do what I do best and not have to learn new things, which is what I dislike, but overall I like the constant variety.

What do you like – or dislike – about working in Tel Aviv?
What I really love about Tel Aviv is the wonderful and supportive ecosystem. As I mentioned before, everyone seems to be founding a startup or working for a startup. When I have a problem I need to solve, I feel like there's always people who want to help, people who have done it before and done it well. For me, it's not about the talents, because they can be found in other places. What makes the Tel Aviv ecosystem special is how much other companies' people are willing to help each other.

[About]   Oribi helps companies understand what drives their business and their users. Unlike most analytics and BI tools, Oribi tells the story of your business without complex integrations and help from developers. Oribi asks the right questions and tells users what they should notice and change.

[Links]   Web: oribi.io Facebook: getoribi Twitter: @getoribi Instagram: oribi_life

Iris Shoor / Oribi

What are your top work essentials?
My dogs – they come to work with me and they're really relaxing.

At what age did you found your company?
I founded my first at twenty-six, and I was thirty-four when I founded Oribi.

What's your most used app?
Probably Slack, and I probably overuse it.

What's the most valuable piece of advice you've been given?
Not to do things by the book. It wasn't specific advice; it was just learning from other entrepreneurs – they don't have strict methodology.

What's your greatest skill?
Probably creativity.

Founders

Oren Simanian

Founder and Venture Partner / StarTAU | Tau Ventures

When Oren Simanian decided in 2007 that Tel Aviv University needed a strong program for entrepreneurs, he thought the best thing to do was to create it himself. He put together a new kind of entrepreneurship center within the university, one designed to support students, alumni and others interested in starting their own ventures. His goal was to promote innovation and entrepreneurship, combining academic, government and private-sector support structures.

How did you get involved in Tel Aviv's startup scene?

Approximately ten years ago, I was studying accounting and economics at Tel Aviv University. I was involved in the more social side of student life at the university, and realized that one of the things missing was a program to nurture young entrepreneurs. Young people have a kind of motivation to create, but they were missing a platform. So in 2007, I had the idea to build up the university's entrepreneurial and business activity. At the time, entrepreneurial life wasn't that sexy. When I compared what already existed at Tel Aviv University to what we could do to support entrepreneurship, I was kind of shocked. I said, "Okay, something is broken here."

So I sat with two of my friends to pick their brains. I knew I wanted to build an entrepreneurship center, a "business" center. I said, "Let's think about a name." So we're throwing names into the air, and my friend Ofer said, "Maybe you take startup and mix TAU [Tel Aviv University] into something. What about StarTAU?" I thought, "Wow, StarTAU is a good name," and then the story began.

How did it grow from there?

I did a lot of research around 2007 and 2008 about what exists in terms of entrepreneurial activities, both at the university and in the private sector. Then I created StarTAU, step by step, without real funding for the first two or three years. It became one of the most well-known anchors of entrepreneurial activity – not only at the university but also in Israel and globally. StarTAU was kind of a model for many other institutes and also for many entrepreneurship centers. It inspired private entrepreneurship centers to develop entrepreneurial activities in communities. To tell the truth, many of them did it even better!

Oren Simanian / StarTAU | TAU Ventures

StarTAU was one of the first and most active entrepreneurial communities in Israel, and still is. One of the strengths it had, and still has, is the ability to think as if it were a private community, even while under the roof of a university. Since then, I've had the ability to grow StarTAU from a Tel Aviv University center to a leading center that sets a lot of the trends and new mechanisms we see on the market, thanks to several factors. First, a great team, as always, is the key to success, as is the ability to work from the bottom up without a budget for the first few years. Second, the university is ranked number eight in the world in terms of entrepreneurship measurements by PitchBook. It's the only non-US university in the top ten worldwide.

What's been the biggest contributor to StarTAU's success?
First, you need to have a strong team. I started StarTAU alone with the support of friends and family, and two students joined about a year later, which created the boost I needed. It's always important to know that you cannot succeed alone; you must have people with complementary skills. With Elad and Elena, and many other team members, we were able to create StarTAU as a strong unit.

Second, from the very first day, the mindset was and still is to be open to all types of students, regardless of their exact studies or what university they study – or studied – at. It allowed us to get exposure to all the talent the city had to offer.

Third, TAU is a leading international university. We used this strength for our entrepreneurial community. In order to succeed in Israel, you have to "act local and think global." Your methods and approach have to translate to the whole international community.

What was the hardest part about starting StarTAU?
Taking the first step. I had to say no to my career as an accountant, and making that decision was 50 percent of the process of starting StarTAU. Second, at the beginning, I didn't have any business model. In other words, I didn't know how to find funding. This was a huge advantage in the end, because we had to create value and invent ourselves in new areas!

Third, the mindset. I'm talking about 2008. It was hard to explain and to market entrepreneurial activities, especially within such a prestigious research university. I'm happy that the president and the VP of R&D gave spiritual support at that time. Now I've been exposed to entrepreneurial activities for nearly ten years, from the government, private

"*Being there in the beginning, being really connected to the ecosystem growth, addressing new market needs and using new methods, has been a real privilege.*"

sector and the university. It's been one of the richest and most fruitful experiences someone can have, especially when we're talking about this entrepreneurial decade, when both young people and all the top-level CEOs and corporate leaders are talking about entrepreneurship, innovation, creativity, open innovation and so on. It's given me a foundation to understand what's going on in the world.

There is a lot of development that we've seen in the last ten years, so being there in the beginning, being really connected to the ecosystem growth, addressing new market needs and using new methods, has been a real privilege. I believe that in order to close the gap and include more people successfully in the startup ecosystem, you need to build methods using GAP – government, academia, private sector – support.

Since you started the center, how has it grown?
Up until 2010, I was just trying to make sure that the center at the university was stable because the first two years I was alone most of the time with the core team, who were all friends and family. The key was the support and the passion Elad and Elena added, and the ability to have Elena take over as CEO after me.

We started in a real "garage": StarTAU was founded in the university bomb shelter. We basically spent something like four years working from a shelter. We reached a point where we were something like eight people who were all working on building entrepreneurship in twelve square meters.

I felt like we'd made a change when Prince Felipe VI of Spain – who is now the king of Spain – visited Israel with his wife. I was still working out of the shelter, and I hosted his team there. I told them the story about what we do, and they were really amazed, not because I had a nice office but by the passion of the people taking part in our activity, and the passion that I reflected in terms of creating a national portal for innovation. So that was a changing point. Sometimes people try to get what you're doing and can't quite grasp it, but once they see that someone else is getting what you're doing, they think to themselves, "If this important guy gets what Oren's doing, maybe there is something there."

StarTAU was a non-profit organization. The idea was to promote entrepreneurship and innovation. The passion was strong, and people didn't come because they thought they were going to get an exit by joining StarTAU, but because they had a passion to create. I continued doing it day by day, sometimes starting at five in the morning and working until eleven at night. Now StarTAU operates in cooperation with the investment structure at Tel Aviv University, TAU Ventures.

Founders

I'm sure that recognition helped. How about the university? What kind of support did it provide?

The president of the university, Professor Joseph Klafter, was always keen to develop innovation and entrepreneurship, even in the first year. I'm sure that he didn't understand what I was doing, but he was so positive because I was passionate about it. Same with the VP of R&D, Professor Ehud Gazit, who supported my initiative; and likewise the chairman of the student union at that time, Mr. Shahar Botzer, who saw the value for TAU students. Over the years, the university allocated seed money and a location, but the spiritual support was more important.

In the beginning, I did tons of small events and presentations to try to convince the faculty, dean by dean. I was meeting with professors too. It takes a lot of energy, you know. And I sometimes asked myself, "Why have I invested so many hours in trying to convince them that it's important to have an entrepreneurship center?" Because it's hard for people to get my point of view. The president gave me something you could call spiritual support. You don't always need money; sometimes you just need someone to say, "Okay, continue. Go on." It was much more important than giving resources and funding. Just the spiritual support.

We still touch base today. We've developed a very active center that has an international department that actually works and communicates with tons of ecosystems around the world, and that makes sure that entrepreneurship is flat – that it reaches everyone and connects people everywhere.

We created one of the biggest and most active engines for entrepreneurial awareness. The apex of that – and the most famous aspect internationally – is the TAU innovation week, which is the biggest early-stage event in Israel. Approximately seven thousand people arrive to network and to share their next ventures.

[About] **StarTAU's** mission is to provide a model that will connect academia, the private sector and government resources so that entrepreneurs and students of entrepreneurship can start successful business ventures. Its training and facilities include workshops, seminars, and unique excellency and mentorship programs with a database of hundreds of mentors and investors.

[Links] Web: startau.co.il Facebook: startau Twitter: @StarTau

Oren Simanian / StarTAU | TAU Ventures

What are your top work essentials?
I have a wall with two thousand business cards. When I need to think about networking, I look at the wall and think who we could use.

At what age did you found your company?
I founded StarTAU at twenty-six.

What's your most used app?
Waze.

What's the most valuable piece of advice you've been given?
Just begin.

What's your greatest skill?
The ability to recognize broken things – areas that need an upgrade.

Founders

Rona Segev

Partner / TLV Partners

Rona Segev studied philosophy at Jerusalem's Hebrew University. At twenty-four, she decided that academia was not for her and moved to Tel Aviv to start her own computer game company, which she sold three years later. She then became a VC and, after a dozen more new companies, acquisitions and IPOs, she cofounded TLV Partners in 2015, a VC firm focusing on B2B software companies.

How did you get into venture capital?
I sold my company at the age of twenty-seven. This was when I was first introduced to the world of VCs. I joined BRM for a year and a half. BRM is managed by some of the top angel investors here in Israel, and I started to learn some of the VC industry, to get to know it. Then in 2000, I joined Evergreen Partners, which was one of the top VCs in Israel back then. I was one of the youngest partners in Israel. They asked me to focus on enterprise software and security. This was in 2001.

I started to invest, and very quickly I had my first exit – in 2003, Actona was sold to Cisco. In 2005, I started to move to Pitango, which was then the largest VC in Israel. They offered me the chance to join as their enterprise software and security partner. I joined them, and some of my companies from Evergreen came to Pitango and wanted me to rejoin their boards and ask Pitango for investment. So I reinvested in Traiana, which was then sold to ICAP for a few hundred million dollars. It's now one of ICAP's largest business units.

I then reinvested in Varonis, which was an investment of mine from Evergreen. Varonis is now a public company on NASDAQ and worth $1.2 billion. I'm still on the board, actually – I'm an independent board member, which has been a very nice ride.

I started investing in lots of different companies. This is also where I met my partner, Eitan Bek, who was also a partner at Pitango. Two and a half years ago, at the beginning of 2015, we decided to start our own fund. The philosophy behind this new fund was that,

first of all, we believe that there is room for early-stage VCs in Israel that focus on helping entrepreneurs build their own companies. Second, we wanted to introduce a new culture in Israel around the collaboration and alignment of interests with a much more relaxed culture. We believe that creating a collaborative culture is a win-win for everyone involved. We've made eight investments so far. The first two are doing very well already; a lot of growth happened after we invested.

If you look at the Israeli ecosystem, you see there's a new generation of VCs that are similar to us in terms of culture and focus. We're very proud to be part of this new generation of VCs that are growing rapidly in Israel. We're attracting a lot of entrepreneurs.

What are the most exciting segments in the Israeli startup scene right now?
There are a lot of segments that Israeli entrepreneurs are really good at. Of course, traditionally there is communication, which is not the sector we're focusing on but has had a lot of success. Then there's security, which is a very successful sector in Israel – more than 30 percent of the market cap of Nasdaq-traded security companies belongs to Israeli companies. Israel is really leading the world in terms of security, and some of the biggest security companies in the world were founded by Israeli entrepreneurs. We're focusing on security as well.

Another area that's becoming very popular in Israel is automotive. Forty percent of the exits that happened in the last few years in the automotive space – probably more than that in terms of value – have come from Israeli companies. Mobileye is of course leading, but there are many others as well.

Cloud computing, too. I can't say it's an area that Israel is leading in the way it leads security and automotive, but there's a lot of expertise in Israel around virtualization. It's an area that we think is going through a dramatic change right now, and it's really interesting for us.

Fintech is another area where Israel is actually a leader. If you look, you see that out of the top fifteen new fintech companies right now, there are five that are Israeli and are leading the pack. The insurance space in particular is going under a lot of change, and we're proud to have one of the leading companies, NextInsurance, in our portfolio. There are other areas that Israel excels at too.

"The most important thing for a startup is to move, rather than freeze – to be constantly moving forward and trying things.... People who have trouble making decisions or moving quickly are often left behind."

Founders

You've worked with a lot of startups. What are some common startup mistakes you've seen?
There are so many mistakes. I think the issue is not making mistakes; making a mistake is actually good, as long as you learn. The most important thing for a startup is to move, rather than freeze – to be constantly moving forward and trying things. You need to reshift your strategy every few months and reposition your company. People who have trouble making decisions or moving quickly are often left behind. So this is one common mistake.

The other thing is not learning from your mistakes and falling in love with your past decisions – not realizing that markets are moving or things are changing, or that you need to change and redefine your company over and over again.

The ecosystem here in Israel has matured tremendously in the past decade. If you asked me that question ten years ago, I'd have said that most of the time people fail because they thought that having the technology is good enough. This is not the case anymore. The Israeli ecosystem is so sophisticated now that most entrepreneurs, even first-time entrepreneurs, understand very quickly that the most important thing is the product, or the product-market fit. And even if they have very good technology behind it, it's a supporting factor but not the main thing.

You've sold quite a few companies. When's the right time for a founder to exit?
There's never a right time. Usually startups that are doing very well will get a lot of acquisition opportunities. The better the company is and the bigger the potential is, the more chances there will be along the way to sell it. The right time to sell is always a mystery, and you'll never know if you made a mistake or not.

I can tell you that on one occasion, we were competing with another company on who would get acquired, and we won. A year afterwards, the company that lost became a $2 billion public company. Looking back, it was a mistake to sell the company at the time, but there were other cases where I'm sure that if we hadn't sold the company it would have been doomed. It really depends on the specific situation of the company. It's one of the toughest decisions you make as a VC or an entrepreneur, to decide when to sell the company and what is the right amount to sell it for.

Founders

What do you like most about working in VC?
I think I'm blessed. I have the best job in the world, really. I get to meet the brightest people in Israel who come to my office for an hour to tell me about new areas and pitch me their brilliant concepts. I'm learning new things every day. So this is one aspect that I really love about this profession.

The other thing I really enjoy is working with people. I think that at the end of the day, this business isn't just about building companies but about building great entrepreneurs. It's a combination of understanding domains and working well with people, and it's fascinating, combining these two elements together.

How is the Tel Aviv ecosystem evolving?
It's growing and maturing rapidly. You'd be shocked at the change from one year to the next. We have a very vibrant community here, a lot of serial entrepreneurs coming from all over the world looking for talent or looking to invest, and people are moving back and forth from Europe and the US. A lot of people are working for international companies and starting their own companies. I think in many ways it resembles Silicon Valley. We're seeing hundreds of startups, and the quality and maturity at even the early stages is amazing.

[About] TLV Partners is a Tel Aviv-based VC firm dedicated to investing in innovative early stage startups. It has a unique and entrepreneur-friendly approach to investing, and looks to truly partner and get involved with the startups it invests in. TLV Partners sees the entrepreneur, not the VC, as the center of the investment, and gets excited by startups that are changing the way things work, the way people think and the shape of the future.

[Links] Web: tlv.partners Facebook: TLV Partners

Rona Segev / TLV Partners

What are your top work essentials?
To be able to concentrate.

At what age did you found your company?
I founded my first company at the age of twenty-four.

What's your most used app?
My CRM and Zapier, which connects many different applications.

What's the most valuable piece of advice you've been given?
Control your ego.

What's your greatest skill?
My ability to learn very quickly.

directory

Startups

Airobotics
7 Simtat HaTavor Street
Petah Tikva
airobotics.co.il

Argus Cyber Security
24 Raoul Wallenberg Street
Tel Aviv-Yafo
argus-sec.com

Biocatch
126 Yigal Alon Street
Tel Aviv-Yafo
biocatch.com

Drupe
18 Abba Eban Boulevard
Herzliya
getdrupe.com

Engie
3 Yokneam Street
Tel Aviv-Yafo
engieapp.com

Feelter
13 Shoken Street
Tel Aviv-Yafo
feelter.com

Hargol FoodTech
4 Bezalel Street
Ramat Gan
hargol.com

HT BioImaging
8 HaBanim 8
Ganei Am
linkedin.com/company/10690472

Lemonade
26 Eliezer Kaplan Street
Tel Aviv-Yafo
lemonade.com

Nexar
58 HaRakevet Street
Tel Aviv-Yafo
getnexar.com

ProoV
2 HaShunit Street
Herzliya
proov.io

Ripples
14 HaMefalsim Street
Petah Tikva
coffeeripples.com

Zest
18 Herzl Street
Ramat Gan
zest.is

Programs

8200 EISP
7 Dubnov Street
Tel Aviv-Yafo
eisp.org.il

The Junction
9 Rothschild Boulevard
Tel Aviv-Yafo
thejunction.co.il

KamaTech
8 Kineret Street
Bnei Brak
kamatech.org.il

MAOF Hybrid
7 Dubnov Street
Tel Aviv-Yafo
thehybrid.io

Microsoft Accelerator
4 Shaul HaMelech Boulevard
Tel Aviv-Yafo
microsoftaccelerator.com

Sigmalabs
19 Tushiya Street
Tel Aviv-Yafo
sigmalabs.co

TechForGood
32 Shoken Street
Tel Aviv-Yafo
techforgood.co

Unistream
26 Harav Shalom Shabazi Street
Rosh Haayin
unistream.co.il

Spaces

AYEKA
26 Elifelet Street
Tel Aviv-Yafo
ayeka.co

Campus Tel Aviv
98 Yigal Alon Street
Tel Aviv-Yafo
campus.co/tel-aviv

Merkspace
121 Dvora HaNevi'a Street
Tel Aviv-Yafo
merkspace.com

Mindspace
54 Ahad Ha'Am Street
Tel Aviv-Yafo
mindspace.me

Sosa
13 Shoken Street
Tel Aviv-Yafo
sosa.co

Spaces
62 Medinat HaYehudim Street
Herzliya
spacesworks.com

WeWork Hazerem
7 HaPelech Street
Tel Aviv-Yafo
wework.com

WMN
121 Dvora HaNevi'a Street
Tel Aviv-Yafo
wmn.co.il

Experts

Microsoft Israel
2 HaPnina Street
Ra'anana
starthub.co.il

Gett
19 HaBarzel Street
Tel Aviv-Yafo
gett.com

useful addresses

Leumi Digital
35 Yehuda Ha-Levi St.
Tel Aviv-Yafo
leumi.co.il

IATI
89 Medinat HaYehudim Street
Herzliya
iati.co.il

Reinhold Cohn & Partners
26 HaBarzel Street
Tel Aviv-Yafo
rcip.co.il

SZ Shvarts Zedkia
54 Ahad Ha'Am Street
Tel Aviv-Yafo
sh-ze.co.il

Founders

Fiverr
8 Eliezer Kaplan Street
Tel Aviv-Yafo
fiverr.com

Mellanox
6 HaBarzel Street
Tel Aviv-Yafo
mellanox.com

NFX Guild
9 HaHoshlim Street
Herzliya
nfx.com

Oribi
33 HaBarzel Street
Tel Aviv-Yafo
oribi.io

OTWOI
40 Einstein Street
Tel Aviv-Yafo
otwoi.com

TLV Partners
21 HaArba'a Street
Tel Aviv-Yafo
tlv.partners

Accountants

Omer Rofe Haim
4 HaTa'asiya Street
Tel Aviv-Yafo
rmr.co.il

Sharon Hezkia
48 Menachem Begin Street
Tel Aviv-Yafo
kh-cpa.co.il

Yehoshua Netanel
4 Koifman Street
Tel Aviv-Yafo
orbaofek.com

Banks

Discount
2 Eliezer Kaplan Street
Tel Aviv-Yafo
discountbank.co.il

Hapoalim
50 Rothschild Boulevard
Tel Aviv-Yafo
bankhapoalim.co.il

Igud
6 Ahuzat Bayit Street
Tel Aviv-Yafo
unionbank.co.il

Leumitech Business center
15 HaManofim Street
Herzliya
leumitech.com

Coffee Shops and Places with Wifi

Arcaffe
17 Ha'Arba'a Street
Tel Aviv-Yafo
arcaffe.co.il

Aroma
22 Rothschild Boulevard
Tel Aviv-Yafo
aroma.co.il

Cafelix
6 Merkhavya Street
Tel Aviv-Yafo
cafelix.de

Java
196 Ben Yehuda Street
Tel Aviv-Yafo
facebook.com/JavaTLV

Landwer
11 Rabenu Tam Street
Tel Aviv-Yafo
landwercafe.co.il

Loveat
3 Nahalat Binyamin Street
Tel Aviv-Yafo
loveat.co.il

The Streets
20 Ashtori Hafarhi Street
Tel Aviv-Yafo
thestreets.co.il

Expat Groups and Meetups

Fuckup Nights
fuckupnightstlv.com

ProductTank TLV
meetup.com/Product-Tank-Tel-Aviv

Startup Grind
startupgrind.com/telaviv

Startup Stadium
facebook.com/StartupStadium

Wize
wize.org.il/he/about-ent

Yazamiot
yazamiyot.com

directory

Flats and Rentals

Komo
komo.co.il

Secret Tel Aviv
secrettelaviv.com

WinWin
winwin.co.il

Yad2
yad2.co.il

Important Government Offices

Invest in Israel
investisrael.gov.il

Ministry of Economy and Industry
economy.gov.il

Ministry of Foreign Affairs
mfa.gov.il

Ministry of Tourism
goisrael.com

National Insurance Institute of Israel
btl.gov.il

Tel Aviv Global & Tourism
tel-aviv.gov.il/en/WorkAnd-Study/Pages/StartupCity.aspx

Incubators

Rad Biomed
radbiomed.com

Samurai House
samurai-incubate-israel.asia

The Time
thetime.co.il

Insurance Companies

Bituach Yashir
555.co.il

Clal
clalbit.co.il

Harel
harel-group.co.il

Menora Mivtachim
menoramivt.co.il

Migdal
migdal.co.il

The Phoenix
fnx.co.il

Investors

2bAngels
32 Shoken Street
Tel Aviv-Yafo
2b-angels.com

Aleph
32 Rothschild Boulevard
Tel Aviv-Yafo
aleph.vc

Canaan Partners Israel
11 HaMenofim Street Building B
Herzliya
canaanil.com

Carmel ventures
12 Abba Eban Boulevard Bldg. D
Herzliya
viola-group.com

Glilot capital
89 Medinat HaYehudim Street
Herzliya
glilotcapital.com

i3 Equity
34 Chaim Levanon Street
Tel Aviv-Yafo
i3equity.com

Lool ventures
2 Tushiya Street
Tel Aviv-Yafo
lool.vc

Mangrove
2 HaShunit Street
Herzliya
mangrove.vc

Pitango
11 HaMenofim Street
Herzliya
pitango.com

Rhodium
91 Medinat HaYehudim Street
Herzliya
rhodium.co.il

Vertex
1 HaShikma Street
Savyon
vertexventures.co.il

YL ventures
54 Ahad Ha'Am Street
Tel Aviv-Yafo
ylventures.com

Language Schools

Berliz
berlitz.co.il

CitizenCafeTLV
citizencafetlv.com

ThisIsNotAnUlpan
thisisnotanulpan.com

Ulpan
jewishagency.org/aliyah/program/302

Ulpanor
ulpanor.com

Ulpanoya
ulpanoya.com

useful addresses

Startup Events

DLD
dldtelaviv.com

IATI MIXiii Biomed 2018
iati.co.il/conference/38

Innovex
innovex.co.il

The Journey
journey-israel.com

Microsoft Tech Summit
microsoft.com/en-il/techsummit/tel-aviv

Marketing and Growth Hackers

Ninja Monkey
ninjamonkey.co.il

Osnat Lidor
osnatlidor.com

Pyro
dreampyro.com

Stardom
stardom.io

Tech News in English

Globes
globes.co.il/en/startups

Israel21c
israel21c.org

Nocamels
nocamels.com

Timesofisrael
timesofisrael.com/start-up-israel

Coding Academies and Software Services

Elevation academy
7 HaPelech Street
Tel Aviv-Yafo
en.elevation.academy

Moveo
1 Har Sinai Street
Tel Aviv-Yafo
moveosoftware.com

Shecodes;
5 HaSolelim Street
Tel Aviv-Yafo
she-codes.org

glossary

A

Accelerator
An organization or program that offers advice and resources to help small businesses grow

Acqui-hire
Buying out a company based on the skills of its staff rather than its service or product

Angel Investment
Outside funding with shared ownership equity

ARR
Accounting (or average) rate of return: calculation generated from net income of the proposed capital investment

B

B2B (Business-to-Business)
The exchange of services, information and/or products from a business to a business

B2C (Business-to-Consumer)
The exchange of services, information and/or products from a business to a consumer

BOM (Bill of Materials)
The list of the parts or components required to build a product

Bootstrap
To self-fund, without outside investment

Bridge Loan
A short-term loan taken out from between two weeks and three years pending arrangement of longer-term financing

Burn Rate
The amount of money a startup spends

Business Angel
An experienced entrepreneur or professional who provides starting or growth capital for promising startups

C

C-level
Chief position

Canvas Business Model
A template for developing new or documenting existing business models

Cap Table
An analysis of the founders' and investors' percentage of ownership, equity dilution and value of equity in each round of investment

CMO
Chief marketing officer

Cold-Calling
The solicitation of potential customers who were not anticipating such an interaction

Convertible Note/Loan
A type of short-term debt often used by seed investors to delay establishing a valuation for the startup until a later round of funding or milestone

Coworking
A shared working environment

CPA
Cost per action

CPC
Cost per click

Cybersecurity
The body of technologies, processes and practices designed to protect networks, computers, programs and data from attack, damage or unauthorized access

D

Deeptech
Companies founded on a scientific discovery or meaningful engineering innovation

Diluting
A reduction in the ownership percentage of a share of stock caused by the issuance of new shares

E

Elevator Pitch
A short summary used to quickly define a product or idea

Exit
A way to transition the ownership of a company to another company

F

Fintech
Financial technology

Flex Desk
Shared desk in a space where coworkers are free to move around and sit wherever they like

I

Incubator
Facility established to nurture young startup firms during their early months or years

Installed Base
A reliable indicator of a platform's popularity

IP (Intellectual Property)
Intangible property that is the result of creativity, such as patents, copyrights, etc

glossary

**IPO
(Initial Public Offering)**
The first time a company's stock is offered for sale to the public

**KPI
(Key Performance Indicator)**
A measurable value that demonstrates how effectively a company is achieving key business objectives

Later-Stage
More mature startups/companies

Lean
Refers to 'lean startup methodology;' the method proposed by Eric Ries in his book for developing businesses and startups through product development cycles

**M&A
(Mergers and Acquisitions)**
A merger is a combination of two companies to form a new company, while an acquisition is the purchase of one company by another in which no new company is formed

MAU
Monthly active user

MVP
Minimum viable product

P

P2P (Peer-to-Peer)
A network created when two or more PCs are connected and sharing resources without going through a separate server

Pitch Deck
A short version of a business plan presenting key figures

PR-Kit (Press Kit)
Package of pictures, logos and descriptions of your services

Pro-market
A market economy/a capitalistic economy

PoC (Proof of Concept)
Evidence demonstrating that a design concept or business proposal is feasible, typically deriving from an experiment or pilot project

Runtime
The amount of time a startup has survived

SaaS
Software as a service

Scaleup
Company that has already validated its product in a market, and is economically sustainable

Seed Funding
First round, small, early-stage investment from family members, friends, banks or an investor

Seed Investor
An investor focusing on the seed round

Seed Round
The first round of funding

Series A/B/C/D
The name of funding rounds coming after the seed stage

Shares
The amount of the company that belongs to someone

Solopreneurs
somebody developing their own personal brand; not a company to hire employees

Startup
Companies under three years old, in the growth stage and becoming profitable (if not already)

SVP
Senior Vice President

Term Sheet/Letter of Intent
The document between an investor and a startup including the conditions for financing (commonly non-binding)

U

Unicorn
A company worth over US$1 billion

USP
unique selling point

**UX
(User experience design)**
The process of enhancing user satisfaction by improving the usability, accessibility and pleasure provided in the interaction between the user and the product

VC (Venture Capital)
Outside venture capital investment from a pool of investors in a venture capital firm in return for equity

Vesting
Employee rights to employer-provided assets over time, which gives the employee an incentive to perform well and remain with the company

203

about the guide

About the Guide

Based on the idea of a traditional guidebook to carry with you everywhere, the guides are made to inspire a generation to become more successful entrepreneurs through case-stories, advice and expert knowledge.
Useful for when you start a project or business, the guide gives insight on where to go, who to talk to and what not to miss from the local people who know the city best.

How we make the guides:
To ensure an accurate and trustworthy guide every time, we team up with a local city partner, ideally an established organization with experience in the local startup scene, who conducts a general call-out to the local community to nominate startups, coworking spaces, founders, incubators and established businesses through an online submission form. These submissions are narrowed down to the top fifty selected companies and individuals. The local advisory board then votes anonymously for the final selection to represent the range of industries and startup stories in the city. The local team, in close collaboration with our editorial and design team in Berlin, then organize and conduct the necessary interviews, photoshoots and research, using local journalists and photographers. All content is then reviewed, edited and approved by the Startup Guide team in Berlin and Copenhagen HQ, who are responsible for the final design, layout and print production.

Who makes the guides:

Sissel Hansen – Founder and CEO
Jenna van Uden – Editor
Josh Raisher – Staff Writer
Marissa van Uden – Copyeditor
Ted Hermann – Proofreader
Tim Rhodes – Production Manager

Ines Pedro – Designer
Daniela Carducci – Photo Editor
Joana Carvalho – Illustrator
João Mira – Marketing and Sales Manager
Eglė Duleckytė – Community and Expansion Manager
Irem Topçuoğlu – Marketing Assistant

Contact us at info@startupguide.world

about the guide

#startupeverywhere

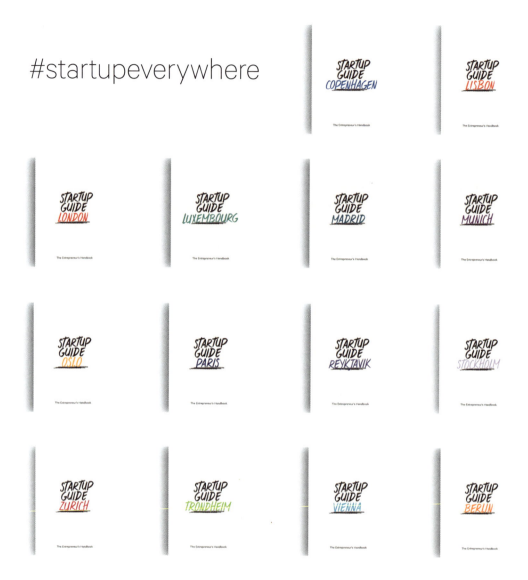

Startup Guide is a creative content and self-publishing company that produces the Startup Guide. We develop, produce and distribute high-quality content and tools to help you navigate in the local and global startup scene. Tailored to aspiring entrepreneurs, founders, freelancers, startups, investors and enthusiasts, it is a place to find inspiration, advice, specific local information and access to a growing network.

Email info@startupguide.world to get in touch with us.

#startupeverywhere

Startup Guide Maps

The perfect navigational companion to the Startup Guide. **Startup Guide Maps** is available on **iOS** and **Android**, and features all the coworking spaces, incubators, accelerators and cafes with wifi for every city that already has a guide.

The Startup Guide Community

Join the global community for entrepreneurs, founders, startups, investors and enthusiasts. Find your local network, get feedback, and access talent, know-how and much more.

The Startup Guide Store

Order a copy online and begin exploring the local startup scenes of Berlin, Copenhagen, Aarhus, Stockholm, Oslo, Lisbon, Trondheim, London and Vienna, with many more to come. You click, we ship.

 ## startupguide.world

Follow us: instagram.com/startupguide.world

Tel Aviv Advisory Board

Avi Domoshevizki
Entrepreneur, Investor and Mentor

Aviv Frenkel
Cofounder and CEO
Enroute

Bat Sheva Moshe
CEO
Unistream

Erez Yerushalmi
Chief Innovation Officer
Avante

Dr. Eyal Benjamin
Head of Entrepreneurship Division
Tel Aviv Yaffo Academic College

Gil Ben-Artzy
Founding Partner
UpWest Labs

Hilla Ovil Brenner
Founder and CEO
Yazamiyot

Itai Kohavi
An Innovator and CEO
Investor and Lecturer

Izhar Shay
Managing General Partner
Canaan Partners Israel

Karin Mayer Rubinstein
CEO and President
IATI - Israel

Lior Elkan
Managing Partner
M-Fund VC

Lior Weizman
Head of Technology Scouting
Deloitte Israel

Dr. Liraz Lasry
Advisor to Investors and Entrepreneurs

Merav Oren
Founder and CEO
WMN and OpenRestaurants™

Roy Oron
Managing Partner
O.G. Tech Ventures

Vered Raviv Schwarz
COO
Fiverr

Yael Elad
CFO
Aleph